The Catholic Church and the Bible

Rev. Peter M. J. Stravinskas

The Catholic Church and the Bible

REVISED EDITION

IGNATIUS PRESS   SAN FRANCISCO

First edition © 1987
Our Sunday Visitor Publishing Division
Our Sunday Visitor, Inc.
All rights reserved
Reprinted with permission

Cover design by Riz Boncan Marsella

Second, revised edition
Printed in 1996 Ignatius Press
ISBN 0-89870-588-6
Library of Congress catalogue number: 96-83640
Printed in the United States of America ∞

CONTENTS

I The Word of the Lord   11

II The Church's Scriptures   27

III A Biblical Theology of the Mass   57

IV Mass Prayers; Biblical Prayers   83

V "What About . . . ?"   107

APPENDICES

A: Catholic Biblical Resources   123

B: Seven Principles Essential to Fundamentalism   129

To the Most Reverend
Paul A. Baltakis, O.F.M.,
Bishop for the Spiritual Assistance
of Lithuanian Catholics of the Diaspora,

On the Occasion
of the 600th Anniversary
of the Christianization of Lithuania:

The Lithuanian nation was the last
in Europe to accept the Word of God;
may she also be the last to relinquish it.

Acknowledgments

Sincere thanks to

Mrs. Sandra Lindstrand
Mr. Walter Petrovitz
Mrs. Loretta Stukas

for their assistance in the careful
preparation of the manuscript and,
more important, for their friendship
and support in so many other ways.

And, for the revised edition,
my deepest gratitude to
the soon-to-be cleric
for the Diocese of Fall River,
Thomas Kocik

I

The Word of the Lord

One of the most persistent and pernicious images of the Church's relationship with the Scriptures is that of the Bible chained to a desk in a medieval library. The image is correct, but the interpretation is not. For critics of the Church, this picture says it all: The Church "chains down" the Word of God both literally and figuratively, placing herself above the Scriptures and at the same time restricting access to the Word.

In point of fact, the image admits of another interpretation—the correct one, I would say, and it is this: The Bible chained to a lectern shows forth the Church's esteem for the Scriptures, as well as her guardianship of them, so that they might be available to the faithful from age to age. But available for what purpose and in what sense? Just how do Catholics regard the Scriptures?

A Catholic Understanding of the Bible

Liberal Protestants, Fundamentalists, and Catholics all speak of the Scriptures as the Word of God (*Catechism of the Catholic Church* 105–8),[1] but each community means something quite

---

[1] References suggesting relevant sections of the *Catechism of the Catholic Church* will hereafter be abbreviated as CCC.

different both in theory and in practice. Perhaps the best guide for discovering the "Catholic" understanding of the Bible is the Dogmatic Constitution on Divine Revelation (Vatican II, *Dei Verbum*).

The Constitution opens with a careful explanation of the basic notions undergirding the process of divine revelation, grounding it in the life and ministry of Jesus, Who "completed and perfected revelation and confirmed it with divine guarantees" (no. 4). Clearly teaching the divine inspiration of the sacred authors and, therefore, the inerrant quality of their writings, the Constitution affirms "that the books of Scripture, firmly, faithfully and without error, teach that truth that God, for the sake of our salvation, wished to be confided to the sacred Scriptures" (no. 11; CCC 107). This serves as a response to a rationalism that would deny the inerrancy of Scripture.

For Fundamentalists or biblical literalists, *Dei Verbum* notes that the interpreter must "carefully search out the meaning that the sacred writers really had in mind, that meaning which God had thought well to manifest through the medium of words" (no. 12; CCC 109). This determination of meaning will come about through an analysis of " 'literary forms, for the fact is that truth is differently presented and expressed in the various types of historical writing, in prophetical and poetical texts' and in other forms of literary expression" (no. 12). In carefully nuanced language, the bishops remind exegetes that correct interpretation involves giving due attention to the historical and cultural milieu in which a particular passage was written (CCC 110). Scripture does not speak for itself, then, but needs both a scientific approach (the work of biblical scholars, along with experts in linguistics, history, archeology, and other allied fields) and a final and authoritative voice. "For, of course, all that has been said about the manner of interpreting Scripture is ulti-mately subject to the judgment of the Church, which exer-cises the divinely conferred commission and ministry of watching over and interpreting the Word of God" (no. 12; CCC 85–87).

While few Catholics are ever tempted to fall into the trap of biblical literalism, not a few have fallen victim to a version of rationalism that would seek to deny the historical truth of the Gospels or the possibility of miracles (even the virginal conception and bodily Resurrection of Jesus). The correct response to such an approach is not a reactionary swing to Fundamentalism (which is equally incompatible with nine-teen centuries of Catholic exegesis) but the "middle road" sketched out by *Dei Verbum*, giving appropriate weight to scientific examination of the Scriptures but done from the perspective of faith and from within the context of the Church's Tradition (CCC 113).

If the Scriptures are inspired by Almighty God and free from error (CCC 105–7), then they should be read. Catholics have always been encouraged to do just that, especially in reference to the Gospels. At the same time, however, the Church has also been concerned that private reading can lead some people to erroneous conclusions. This problem is faced squarely in the Acts of the Apostles when Philip asks the Ethiopian eunuch if he understands the Scriptures he is read-ing. Unashamed, the man says, "How can I, unless someone instructs me?" (Acts 8:27–39). In other words, the Bible is not self-explanatory, and the concerns of the Church are not un-founded. The solution is not to avoid private reading but to engage in such reading with prudence and caution, making use of good commentaries and guides, including one's parish priest. Of course, the most beneficial reading of Scripture ideally occurs in the liturgical assembly (CCC 132) as the

Church comes together to hear God's Word proclaimed and explained.

But in all candor we must ask: How free are Catholics not only to read the Bible but to interpret it? At the risk of sounding flippant, I would say as free as any non-Catholic Christian. Martin Luther began as an advocate of private scriptural interpretation, reasoning that if the Pope can interpret the Bible, why not he or any other Christian? Luther's speeches and letters show that later in life he backed off from this position after seeing the disastrous results of having unprepared and unqualified people give personal reactions to the Bible, allegedly of equal value to the contributions of scholars. Furthermore, most Protestant denominations have very defined explanations of critical passages, not allowing much leeway for their members' private judgment, whether the issues might be the significance of water baptism, faith and works, divorce and remarriage, or the Eucharist.

That said, one should note that Catholics are really quite uninhibited in this process. They are instructed to read a given passage according to the manifest intent of the sacred author (CCC 109), which intention usually becomes clear from the context of the entire book. If that fails to yield conclusive results, a Catholic consults the accumulated wisdom of the Church. Vatican II put it this way:

> The task of an authentic interpretation of the Word of God, whether written or handed on, has been entrusted exclusively to the living teaching office of the Church alone. Its authority in this matter is exercised in the name of Jesus Christ. Yet this Magisterium is not superior to the Word of God, but is its servant. It teaches only what has been handed on to it. At the divine command and with the help of the Holy Spirit, it listens to this devotedly, guards it with dedication and expounds

it faithfully. All that it proposes for belief as being divinely revealed is drawn from this single deposit of faith (*Dei Verbum*, no. 10; CCC 95).

A skeptic may pounce on this as proof that the Church suppresses personal reflection, but history attests to the contrary. Father Raymond Brown, writing in the *Jerome Biblical Commentary* (the best single guide available for Scripture study), categorically asserts that "the Church has the power to determine infallibly the meaning of Scripture in matters of faith and morals"; however, he immediately goes on to note that this never involves technicalities like authorship or dating of a book. In point of fact, the Church exercises great restraint in offering authoritative interpretations of individual pericopes (texts); fewer than a dozen such instances can be pointed to in her two-thousand-year history, most of them at the Council of Trent.

For example, the Church has declared that Calvin was wrong in seeing John 3:5 as a mere metaphor. Equally condemned are those who would deny any link between John 20:23 and the sacrament of penance. The reader will note that both instances do not give definitive, positive interpretations but simply call into question an interpretation that has been advocated.

From a positive vantage point, the Church has declared Matthew 16:17f. and John 21:15 as germane to the doctrine of Petrine primacy, and James 5:14 as tied in to the sacrament of the sick. Likewise, the Church has indicated the Gospel accounts of the institution of the Eucharist are to be literally understood.

So few examples can hardly be perceived as a heavy-handed attempt to stifle private interpretation. It is also worth noting that whenever a rare, definitive interpretation is given, it is done only after consultation with the best exegetes of the day, as well as allowing for the divine guidance promised by Jesus to His Church (see Jn 14:26, 16:13). To push for one's own interpretation counter to twenty centuries of authentic and authoritative understanding of a particular passage would appear to be spiritual pride and arrogance of the worst sort. Just as the books of the Bible were collected into one by the Church, so too ought one to read that Bible as a member of that same Church (CCC 113).

To put it in the simplest terms possible, Catholics see the Bible as a work to be read, studied, prayed over and with, using both their heads and hearts to gain the deepest knowledge of the Lord, Who offers His Word as a means of sharing His life.

Scripture and Tradition

Which comes first, the chicken or the egg? That question can touch off an endless debate because it is largely irresolvable.

In the realm of theology some questions have a similar effect. For many, the question "Which comes first, Scripture or Tradition?" is equally impossible to resolve. A careful analysis of the question, however, yields a very clear and satisfactory answer.

Some definitions are in order at the outset. Sacred Scripture, or the Bible, is that collection of works written under divine inspiration. Sacred Tradition is the unwritten or oral record of God's Word to His prophets and apostles, received under divine inspiration and faithfully transmitted to the Church under the same guidance. Tradition differs from Scripture in that Tradition is a living reality passed on and preserved in the Church's doctrine, life, and worship, while Scripture is a tangible reality found in written form (CCC 81–82).

Since the Protestant Reformation, a sticking point in ecumenical dialogue has been the perceived rivalry between Scripture and Tradition. The way *Dei Verbum* handles the problem, the conflict is more apparent than real, as the bishops declare that "sacred Tradition and sacred Scripture make up a single sacred deposit of the Word of God, which is entrusted to the Church" (no. 10; CCC 80, 84). Thus is the focus of the debate shifted from one of "Scripture versus Tradition" to a discussion of the Lord's desire to reveal Himself to His people, a process carried forward by both Scripture and Tradition.

From the temporal point of view, Tradition precedes Scripture (CCC 83), and the Church precedes both, in that the writing of the New Testament did not begin until some fifteen to twenty years after the Pentecostal formation of the Church and was not completed until perhaps as late as A.D. 120. The Gospel message, then, was imparted through oral tradition first, and only later was it committed to written form. The means (whether oral or written), however, is in many ways secondary to the goal (revelation) and to the receiver of the revelation (God's people, the Church).

An example from American government might be instructive. The law of the land is found in the Constitution of the United States; it is normative for American life. However, it is not a self-interpreting document. On the contrary, it calls for detailed, professional interpretation from an entire branch of government dedicated to that purpose. Furthermore, when conflicting views do emerge, standard procedures of jurisprudence call for a return to the sources, in an effort to discover the mind of the people who produced the document.

With appropriate allowances made for the divine workings in the case of Scripture, Tradition, and the Church, one finds many parallels that are useful. First, the Scriptures did not descend from heaven in final form but took shape in and through the community of the Church, responding to and working under divine inspiration. Second, the Scriptures are not self-explanatory documents but require "an authentic interpretation", which task "has been entrusted to the living, teaching office of the Church alone" (CCC 85), according to the Second Vatican Council. The bishops conclude these considerations by asserting that "in the supremely wise arrangement of God, sacred Tradition, sacred Scripture and the Magisterium of the Church are so connected and associated that one of them cannot stand without the others. Working together, each in its own way under the action of the Holy Spirit, they all contribute effectively to the salvation of souls" (*Dei Verbum*, no. 10).

Is this explanation mere wishful thinking to justify Catholic theology and practice? Not at all, for the historical record bears out all these points. The canon of the Bible (the officially accepted list of inspired books) is the clearest proof of the validity of this approach (CCC 120). We know with the utmost certitude that no authoritative list of scriptural books existed until the fourth century. And who then produced this canon? None other than the Church meeting in ecumenical council. Therefore, the value and even, one could say, the validity of the written Word is established only after its inspiration and inerrancy are assured and attested to by the Church. The process of divine revelation thus began with the Church, through Tradition, and subsequently passed into Scripture, and not the other way around.

Can it happen, though, that Scripture and Tradition will at times contradict each other? Impossible—because they are just two sides of the same coin, whose purpose is the same and whose origins are the same. Since God wishes to reveal Himself to us, He has guaranteed the process in both its oral and written expressions (and not one more than the other). Furthermore, God cannot contradict Himself. Saint Paul apparently had this very concept in mind when he urged his readers at Thessalonika to "hold fast to the traditions that you were taught, either by an oral statement or by a letter of ours" (2 Th 2:15). This very passage, however, raises a secondary but related problem.

Some Christians tend to confuse "Tradition" with "traditions" (CCC 83). Having already defined Tradition, we need to consider the meaning and place of traditions (customs or practices). Sacred Tradition is divine in origin and, so, unchangeable; traditions are human in origin and therefore changeable. Some examples that come to mind are various devotions to the saints, processions, acts of penance, and the use of incense or holy water. No Church authority has ever held that these practices are divinely mandated; at the same time no one can demonstrate that they are divinely forbidden. Traditions exist to put people in touch with Almighty God. To the extent that they do, they are good; to the extent that they do not, they are bad and should be modified or abolished.

Certain defined dogmas, on the other hand, cannot be found explicitly in Scripture (for example, Mary's Assumption or Immaculate Conception), yet the Church binds her members to an acceptance of these teachings. How so? First of all, because nothing in Scripture contradicts these dogmas. Second, because they have been a part of the Tradition (or oral revelation) from the very beginning. Third, because they can be implicitly located in Scripture, waiting, in a sense, to be uncovered by the Church's prayerful reflection over the centuries.

Scripture comes alive only in the life of the community that gave it birth and has ever since preached and proclaimed it (CCC 94). To remove Scripture from its moorings in the Church is to deny it genuine vitality. Scripture provides Tradition with a written record against which to judge its fidelity and thus serves as a safeguard. In the "balance of powers" (to resort once more to the governmental analogy), Tradition is a defense against an unhealthy individualism that distorts the Bible through a private interpretation at odds with the constant Tradition of the Church.

For Christians, the Bible is not revelation in itself; for us, revelation is a Person, not a book—no matter how holy. To worship a book is bibliolatry. A truly accurate and truly Christian view of revelation takes all these seriously: God, the Church, the Church's Tradition, and the Church's Scriptures. The focus of our attention, however, is not the Church, the Scriptures, or Tradition, but God. The other three are means given to us to arrive at our end—union with God (CCC 95).

Sacred Scripture in the Life of the Church

"The Church has always venerated the divine Scriptures as she venerated the Body of the Lord", begins the sixth chapter of Vatican II's *Dei Verbum* (CCC 141), as the bishops endeavored to situate Scripture in the life of the Church. Many non-Catholic Christians would question the accuracy of this Vatican II assertion. It is the purpose of this chapter (and indeed of this entire book) to demonstrate that the Catholic Church is not only a "Bible-based" Church but *the* Bible-based Church. As Alfred Emmanuel Smith was fond of putting it, "Let's look at the record."

From time immemorial, the Church has served as the guardian and preserver of the Scriptures. And why not? For it was she who mothered the New Testament (CCC 124–27), and it was she who authoritatively determined just which books should be included in the canon of the Bible (CCC 120). The Church has always sought to expose her sons and daughters to God's Word by the most appropriate means possible. In times of low literacy, that was best accomplished through preaching and teaching that concentrated on the key persons and events of Bible history, especially those that had their origin in the life and ministry of our Lord, as they are handed on in the Gospels.

Salvation history was passed on for centuries through the Church's liturgical arts in stained-glass windows (known in art history as "the bible of the poor"), paintings, sculpture, and hymns. For most American Catholics over thirty, grammar-school religion classes involved not only the Baltimore Catechism but also serious and extensive study of Bible history. Since Vatican II, the methodology has shifted so that young Catholics study the Bible itself and not merely about the Bible. This development resulted from the Church's confidence that a sufficiently educated laity was emerging that could profit immeasurably from direct exposure to the Scriptures through private reading and formal guided study (CCC 133). The Church's only historical hesitancy has been a fear that private reading of Scripture could lead an untrained reader to erroneous and harmful conclusions—which has happened often enough in the past twenty years to be a source of genuine concern but not often enough to discourage the practice. To prevent such misfortunes from occurring, the Church encourages believers to engage in Bible study groups (now commonplace in parishes around the country) or in formal classes, so that one's personal reading of the Bible can be buoyed by the necessary background information in history, archaeology, linguistics, and theology. Few students can attend a Catholic high school or college and fail to have heavy doses of such courses. While seminary education always involved the study and use of Scripture in regular courses in exegesis and preaching, as well as in the areas of dogmatic and moral theology and liturgy, the use of Scripture in contemporary Catholic seminary training might conceivably outstrip its use in most similar Protestant courses of study (CCC 132).

However, it is important to observe that Catholic biblical scholarship is not a twentieth-century phenomenon, nor did the Church enter this arena as a grudging participant or "Johnny-come-lately". On the contrary, the Fathers and Doctors of the Church were the very people who began biblical study in earnest. Their letters, lectures, and homilies—beginning in the first century and continuing up to modern times—provide clear historical evidence of the Church's continuous efforts to make God's Word intelligible and profitable to God's people.

Saint Jerome worked with the Sacred Scriptures in the fourth century, having prepared himself for his lifelong task by a careful study of all the ancient languages and by visiting (and living in) the key spots highlighted in the Bible, especially those connected with the life of Christ. Another great biblical scholar, Saint Augustine, praised Jerome's erudition by remarking that "what Jerome is ignorant of, no mortal has ever known". His commentaries on Scripture still provide valuable and valid insights into the meaning of debated, controversial, or confusing texts. His real claim to fame, however, rests in his monumental achievement of translating the entire Bible into Latin, a translation known as the Latin Vulgate. At times, critics of the Church hold the Latin Vulgate up as proof that the Church was intent on keeping the Scriptures away from the average believer. This is to miss the very point of the Vulgate, which was designed to take the Scriptures out of the obscure and scholarly languages of Hebrew and Greek and to render them into a tongue understandable to the common people, hence Jerome's choice of "vulgar" Latin, the Latin universally known and used at that time.

In the Middle Ages, the Bible was preserved through the painstaking efforts of the monks, who not only copied the biblical texts by hand but also the commentaries of the early Church Fathers. It is no exaggeration to suggest that if it were not for the medieval Church, there would have been no Scriptures around which Martin Luther could rally with his slogan of *sola Scriptura* ("Scripture alone").

At the Council of Trent, the bishops called for improvements to be made in Jerome's Vulgate, as did Pope Pius XII in this century. With the gradual emergence of modern languages, vernacular translations began to appear and to be accepted by the Church. The three English translations most frequently used by Catholics in the United States are the Jerusalem Bible, the New American Bible, and the Catholic edition of the Revised Standard Version—all approved by competent ecclesiastical authority.

In addition to scholarly biblical journals, Catholic publishers make available periodicals of a more popular nature, as well as concordances, commentaries, and biblical dictionaries and encyclopedias—all to enable Catholics to read the Scriptures in a way that does justice to the texts and brings life and holiness to the reader. Before Jerome and since, the Church has profited from the learning of people who have committed their whole lives to the advancement of biblical study. To this day, the most difficult and prestigious ecclesiastical degree is the doctorate in Sacred Scripture obtained from the Pontifical Biblical Commission or Institute in Rome or the École Biblique in Jerusalem.

All the foregoing information might be interesting, but it could all apply to less than a sizable portion of the whole Church.

What kind of an impact does this scholarly activity have on the average person in the pew? Well, it is precisely that Catholic in that very spot who does receive the benefits of the Catholic devotion to the Bible.

If a Catholic were to read no Scripture beyond the passages used for Sunday Mass over the three-year cycle, that person would have been exposed to more than seven thousand verses of the Bible—no mean accomplishment. Of course, Bible reading has always formed the first half of the Mass (CCC 1154–55, 1190, 1349) from apostolic times (as the New Testament attests), but the lectionary revised in response to the liturgical renewal of Vatican II opened up even more of the Bible to the Sunday-Mass Catholic. The new lectionary is so extensive in its coverage of nearly the entire New Testament and most significant portions of the Old Testament over a three-year period that most mainline Protestant denominations have adopted it. If a Catholic attends daily Mass, the percentage of Scripture taken in over a two-year span is more than double that for the Sunday readings.

Catholics have often been intimidated into thinking that Fundamentalists read more of the Bible than Catholics, but this is not necessarily true—either quantitatively or qualitatively, especially qualitatively. Most Fundamentalist ministers select biblical passages according to the topic they wish to handle for a particular day; it is not unusual for them to have "pet" themes and "pet" passages, to which their congregations are treated on a recurring basis. This kind of eclectic or selective Bible reading is not possible in Catholic liturgy, because the readings are assigned to a given day. Thus, the sermon or homily must flow from the Word of God; the cleric's biases or interests do not determine the sections of the Word of God to be proclaimed. This is not an insignificant point to understand and appreciate.

Aside from the obvious Scripture readings that form the backbone of the Liturgy of the Word, the Mass is a thoroughly biblical prayer: in the direct scriptural citations, in the paraphrases, and in the biblical allusions. The Mass begins and ends with quotations from Scripture: "The Lord be with you" (said several times in the course of the Mass) comes from the Book of Ruth, as the alternate greetings come from the writings of Saint Paul. The dismissal rite, "Go in peace", adopts the words commonly used by our Lord after performing His miracles.

Everything else sandwiched in between can be found to originate in the life and ministry of the Lord Jesus Himself. The Offertory prayers (CCC 1350) are based on the traditional Hebrew words of benediction used by Christ at the Last Supper. Eucharistic Prayer I abounds in biblical allusions to Abel, Abraham, and Melchizedek. Eucharistic Prayer IV is nothing more or less than a complete summation of salvation history. At the heart of every Mass are repeated the texts of our Lord's words of institution of the Eucharist, found in all three Synoptic Gospels (CCC 1352–53).

The Communion Rite begins with the Lord's Prayer as recorded in the Gospel according to Saint Matthew (CCC 2759–865). The Rite of Peace quotes Saint John's Gospel and is followed by the breaking of the bread, the expression used for the Mass in the Acts of the Apostles; the prayer is a direct quotation of John the Baptist's witness to Jesus. Christ is acknowledged as truly present by the congregation in the words of the Roman centurion, who asserted his own unworthiness to have Christ come under his roof.

The reception of Holy Communion is as old as Christianity itself, beginning at the Lord's Last Supper; Christians have always understood our Lord to be really and substantially present in the Eucharist, since Christ challenged those who did not do so to leave Him, as the first skeptics did (see Jn 6:67; CCC 1384).

The vestments, vessels, gestures, preaching, and sacrificial offering of the Mass today are so thoroughly biblical that it would not be rash to assert that if one of the Twelve were to enter a Catholic church during Mass any day, he would understand completely what was under way.

If it were possible to have too much of a good thing, this brief survey of the average Catholic's involvement with the Scriptures might suggest that he is supersaturated with the Bible, for it truly permeates a Catholic's life both in private and public worship. The Fathers of Vatican II, then, did not engage in hyperbole by declaring that Catholics venerate the Scriptures just as they venerate the Lord's Body, for the Word must always take on flesh—one logically leading to the other (CCC 103).

II

The Church's Scriptures

If we were to seek an apt image to describe the God of the Bible, it might well be Francis Thompson's "Hound of Heaven", relentlessly pursuing man, seeking to persuade him to enter into a love affair with his God (CCC 142). The Bible is the story of that encounter between God and a certain people He calls His own (Israel and the Church). It is an encounter that occurs in ordinary human events and in not-so-ordinary events, but it is concrete and real. The Judeo-Christian Tradition takes most seriously God, man, and human history; those of us who share this common Tradition must have a similar appreciation, for the religion of the Bible presupposes such a prior understanding.

One question that is very basic to our entire consideration is: Why study Scripture? Whole books have been written to answer that question, but let me simply suggest some directions we might take. First of all, it is fundamental to our faith that God wishes to reveal Himself. He does not delight in obscurity but wants us to know Him (CCC 54). He consistently makes overtures of this nature in the Old Testament (CCC 121–23); in the New Testament He reveals Himself most definitively in the person of His Son (CCC 124). If God is so anxious to make known His identity, we should be equally anxious to learn (CCC 203ff.).

Secondly, we believe that the Scriptures are the Word of God (CCC 135). The "word" was a powerful concept to a Hebrew; it was a part of the speaker, an extension of the self. The word was creative: "By the word of the LORD the heavens were made" (Ps 33:6). Nor is God's Word a relic of history; it "is living and effective, sharper than any two-edged sword" (Heb 4:12).

If God's Word is intimately connected with Him, it must be true and profitable for us to give ear to it.

The Scriptures give us an insight into our heritage and provide us with an identity. Every Christian is a religious Semite, which is to say that the Christian faith builds on the foundation of the religion of Israel. To be unaware of Jewish religion, thought, and history is to miss out on much of the meaning of Christianity.

The Bible is a record of God's love and mighty deeds from which we receive consolation and inspiration, for it is here that we see God acting on behalf of His people and making His promises. If God is God, He is faithful to His promises. If He acted then, He will act now. Therein lies our reason for hope.

How to Study Scripture

Read the Bible as a member of the Church (CCC 94, 133). This implies many things. First, seek the company of other interested people and the guidance of a priest; both are great assets in Bible study. Second, realize that God is speaking to you as part of a community, the community that wrote the Scriptures under divine inspiration. Third, recall that God's basic desire is to gift you with His presence. He does this in many ways: through the Tradition of the Church, through the sacraments, through personal prayer and everyday occurrences. In other words, do not fall prey to a biblicism or fundamentalism that sees the Bible as having the definitive word on every subject. God never intended it for that. The living Church, in her constant search to understand the meaning of God's Word, is the best guide to an enjoyable and fruitful encounter with the God Who reveals Himself in the events of Scripture (CCC 98).

Although many people try to complicate the process, the study of Scripture can be relatively simple. First of all, the desire to study Scripture provides an incentive and impetus in itself. Reading the Word of God prayerfully with reflection is a very powerful form of communication with God. Throughout the seventy-three books that comprise the Bible, the message of the Scriptures is very clear and touched upon in a multitude of ways: God is the Savior (CCC 107, 128–30).

It is important to obtain a reliable translation of the Bible, one that has good explanatory notes. While there may be a certain mystique about archaic language, it does much to obscure the meaning of the text. Good options for American Catholics include the following: New American Bible,[1] Revised Standard Version,[2] and Jerusalem Bible. All three have corresponding lectionaries approved for liturgical use.

As can be seen already, selecting an English translation has been complicated in the past decade by an additional problem, heretofore unknown, namely, the drive in certain quarters for so-called "inclusive language."

---

[1] The original edition of 1970 is good, as is the 1986 edition, which contains a revision of the New Testament; the latest edition to appear has a revised Psalter that is extremely problematic.

[2] Again, it is important to check publication dates. The original Catholic edition (1965) is excellent and has been reprinted by Ignatius Press; the 1993 revision is seriously defective.

As many readers know, "political correctness" has invaded some segments of the Church, with the consequence that theology has taken a back seat to ideology—and often an ideology that subtly and sometimes even directly destroys the integrity of the Catholic Faith. While no one should deliberately use language designed to hurt or alienate people, several points about "inclusive language" need to be noted to place in context any discussion of it.

First, living languages change, to be sure, but they do so normally and organically—not by fiat of some thought- or speech-patrol bureau. "Inclusive language" has not emerged naturally; nor was anyone ever consulted to determine whether women or anyone else felt marginalized by standard English usage.

Which leads to our second point: A select group of people, claiming to represent the majority, have attempted to orchestrate a groundswell of opposition to the generic use of words like "man", "mankind", and "men", as well as the use of "he" as a resumptive, generic pronoun—with the summary declaration that all these (and many other words, patterns of speech, and expressions as well) are "sexist". Human speech, then, has become a source of politicization and conflict. But to what end?

This brings us to a third aspect of the question: linguistic engineering is seen as a prelude to social engineering. In other words, proponents of "inclusive language" have a very clear agenda for society in general and the Church in particular. Although they are not pleased with the reminder, it is good to recall that both Hitler and Mussolini deemed linguistic changes essential to the success of their programs of reform or revolution.

Fourth, reasonable people will be comfortable with the fact that all languages have inherent weaknesses. For the sake of discussion, let us grant that in English, having a generic pronoun with the same form as the masculine is one such weakness. Why is it, however, that men (that is, males) in countries that use any of the Romance languages are not in revolt over aspects of their native tongues that discriminate against themselves (for example, the word for "person" is feminine and requires a feminine pronoun to follow)? The truth of the matter, of course, is that males in those places are no more exercised about that alleged problem than are the majority of females in the English-speaking world about the generic use of "man" or "he".

Last but not least, when language is seen as the bearer of concepts of Christian faith, one must be especially cautious. Some renditions of the psalms, for instance, arbitrarily make singular masculine pronouns into plurals, bringing about the near-total elimination of a possible christological interpretation of these prayers—a method of exegesis of these sacred poems that goes back to the very origins of Christianity.[3] While this excursus on "inclusive language" is, for some, tedious and tangential, I think it is important to warn the unsuspecting of some of the minefields they could enter.

Old Testament Themes

The Old Testament is a massive collection of forty-six books that recount historical events that date from approximately 1800 B.C. While it may make one proud to boast, "I have read

[3] Yet another factor to weigh is the responsibility of a translator to attempt to provide as objective and faithful a text from one language to another. For example, if the sacred author utilized a singular, can one deem himself authorized to make it a plural? Even more serious is that some translations of Scripture have taken third person singular pronouns ("he") and rendered them as second person plurals ("you") or third person plurals ("they")—all to expunge "he" from the final text!

every book of the Bible", do not feel compelled to read the Bible in its entirety. Read what interests you. The Old Testament books can be divided into historical, prophetical, and wisdom literature (CCC 120).

The historical books record the deeds of God in establishing and protecting His people, Israel. They also recall the failures of this people. Of these books, the first five (the Pentateuch, or Torah) are most important. In Genesis we encounter a theological poem attempting to explain the marvels of creation, and we see God's care and providence extend to the forming of a very special people, Israel (CCC 289–90, 62–64). Exodus celebrates the deliverance of a people and the birth of a nation (CCC 130). Leviticus shows us the holy nature of this nation; Numbers delineates that nation's organization. Deuteronomy gives the law and the spirit of this community: love (see Dt 6:4–5). If the reader of the Old Testament comes away with even the most basic notion that the God of the Old Testament was not an angry God but the same God of love Jesus preached and encouraged us to address as "Father", then his reading would have had one very positive effect.

The prophetical books are challenges to a people who failed their God, and as such these books are quite appropriate for us as well. They encourage the faithful and rebuke the backsliders. There is also in these writings an element of foretelling, but it is not the overriding theme; it was really used to give the assurance needed for men to return to God.

The wisdom literature is a prayerful reflection of the devout on the deeds of God in history and in their own lives. These books make beautiful reading because they are charged with love, emotion, and faith. They stem from real-life experiences and have an abiding refrain, which may be summarized as: "Happy the man who follows not the counsel of the wicked nor walks in the way of sinners, nor sits in the company of the insolent, but delights in the law of the LORD and meditates on his law, day and night" (Ps 1:1). It is the collective wisdom of a nation that has grown old with God and now realizes where true wisdom lies.

As Christians, we always read the Old Testament with the New Testament in view. And this is quite correct, because the New Testament is the culmination of God's saving work begun in the Old Testament. Saint Augustine said: "The New Testament is hidden in the Old, and the Old becomes clear in the New." What this Father of the Church was trying to say is that the two Testaments are interrelated and mutually dependent. Furthermore, the focal point of revelation is the person of Jesus Christ, and we must always keep Him in mind when reading the Scriptures. Therefore, it is very beneficial to take some specific themes of the Old Testament and to trace them through to the New Testament (CCC 129).

Covenant

The covenant was a very ancient form of pact, treaty, or testament in which the parties pledged themselves to mutual support and assistance. The idea was that both parties had something to offer and that their combined efforts would be of more account than their individual endeavors. Covenants were made for purposes of commerce, war, and the like. Rights were recognized, and obligations were established.

In the Scriptures, we find God committing Himself to such an agreement. What is utterly fantastic about this is the fact that there is no equality between God and man; man has nothing to offer God, yet God wishes to establish such a relationship with him.

The first covenant we encounter is the one with Adam. God gave Adam everything: the only stipulation was that he obey (see Gen 2:16f.). Failure to obey would result in a severing of the pact, and death would come about. Man did not live up to the bargain, and the covenant was broken. Yet, even in the midst of disaster, God promised to undo the damage and to reestablish his ties with man through the one who would conquer evil (Gen 3:15).

God next chose to favor Abram (Abraham) with the opportunity for him and his descendants to share in the rewards of faith and obedience (CCC 59–61). God promised Abraham posterity (Gen 12:2), Palestine (12:7), and the blessings of His protection (12:3). For his part, Abraham was to walk with his God in justice and faith. This covenant was everlasting; nothing could undo it. Its sign and reminder to man would be circumcision. That covenant put Abraham in a position of familiarity with God (see Gen 18:17ff.). This pact was with a family, but it was destined to encompass a whole nation and, eventually, all humanity.

This began to happen when the promise made to Abraham was extended to Israel as a whole, provided that they kept the commandments of the Lord (see Ex 19:5; CCC 709, 751). The Sinai covenant elaborates on the pact with Abraham and provides even greater opportunity for intimacy with God, for the Lord dwells with His people (see Ex 40:34ff.; CCC 697). However, the people still fail, so that God must continuously remind them of their obligations.

And so it was throughout Israel's history that the nation had to be reminded of God's eternal love (Jer 31:3; CCC 220), even though they failed to live up to His love (Is 54:10). Therefore, the prophet could be confident of God's continued mercy and faithfulness to His people and to His covenant (Micah 7:20). Still other prophets looked at God's covenant love and saw in it the fidelity of a faithful spouse. Israel, on the other hand, was compared to an adulterous spouse who leaves her God for other gods (see Hos 2:19, Jer 3:1–5, Ex 16:6ff.). As an exhortation to faithfulness, Israel observed days of covenant renewal in which the people were reminded of God's tremendous love and were urged to respond with loving obedience.

Fidelity to the covenant was also of political importance because the bond that held the community of Israel together was the covenant.

By keeping to the covenant, Israel was to be a light to all the nations (Is 42:6). Thus, God's power and glory would be revealed to the Gentiles. By seeing God's goodness to Israel, the nations too would believe, and so, through Israel, all nations would be blessed as God had promised to Abraham (Gen 12:3; CCC 59).

The absoluteness and complete perfection of God's covenant with man reached perfection when it was made in Christ's blood for all people of all time (see Mk 14:23f.; CCC 706). All former covenants found their fulfillment in this one covenant (Heb 8; CCC 1965ff.). In his two beautiful canticles, Luke has Mary and Zechariah (1:46–55, 68–79) sing of the coming of Christ as the decisive event in the history of God's promises to Abraham and his descendants.

The Kingdom of God (CCC 541–56)

What was the real purpose of the covenant? It was to bring about the Kingdom of God, God's rule over all human hearts. While the term "Kingdom of God" is not widely used in the Old Testament, it is the desired goal of Israel's existence. Through observance of the law, Israel would enjoy prosperity and peace. Looking at her, other nations would be drawn to the worship of the one true God, and thus the Kingdom would be begun.

The Kingdom of God involved the acceptance of God's will by all men, a revolutionary change in mankind's attitudes—and even in nature itself (CCC 2822–27). It would be entirely new. Because the Israelites always thought in very concrete ways, they looked to the Kingdom of God for universal peace (Is 2:1f.), the elimination of injustice (Is 32), and an end to death (Is 25:8). It would also be characterized by the knowledge of God (Is 11:9), holy subjects (Ezek 36:25–28), perfect worship (Zech 4), and religious universalism (Is 19:23–25). Likewise, many of the psalms look toward and praise that day when God's Kingdom will be established in these terms (see Ps 46, 92, 96, 98, 149).

Since Judaism at that time did not have a clear teaching on the afterlife, these earth-shattering events were seen as occurring within history, ending a former era and introducing a new one. Even judgment took place within the scheme of human affairs as God met and conquered men's resistance, for judgment came to be viewed as a saving act by many.

One of the surest aspects of the preaching of Jesus revolved around the Kingdom of God, which He inaugurated and which will be discussed more fully in another section. For the present, let us mention that Jesus saw the Kingdom as a spiritual reality already present (see Lk 17:21; CCC 2816), which demanded childlike faith for entrance and membership (see Mk 10:14f.).

The Messiah (CCC 436–40)

The Kingdom of God would come about, in Jewish thinking, through the Messiah, God's anointed one. This king would be a party to the covenant and would be responsible for it. By his faithfulness, he would be a son of God. Thus, an entire dynasty became conscious of its messianic vocation. Because of his role in establishing the Kingdom of God, he received God's special assistance. Therefore, the day of enthronement also became the day of his divine adoption: "You are my son; this day I have begotten you" (Ps 2:7).

Throughout much of Israel's history, it seems that the Messiah was seen as a king or a political figure. Even the famous oracles in Isaiah had their original setting in the imminent expectation of a king. The Church, in reading the Scriptures, perceived a deeper meaning in these prophecies (Is 7:14, 9:6, 11:1–4) and saw them admirably fulfilled in the person of Jesus, Whose message of love will ultimately enable the wolf to be a guest of the lamb (Is 11:6), thus bringing about the total harmony that the Kingdom of God is destined to be.

As it became increasingly obvious that the kings were not living up to their vocation, many in Israel began to turn to others for a Messiah, such as the one we find described in the "Servant Songs" of Isaiah 42 and 49–53. This Servant would suffer and, through his sufferings, justify many. He would bear the guilt of the people. Because of his faithfulness, he would be exalted.

It seems that Jesus did not readily accept the title of "Messiah" because it was so clouded over with worldly associations that would detract from His central mission; its use may have also linked Him too closely with Israel alone. Jesus regarded Himself as a servant and appears to have accepted only the messianic titles of "Son of David" and "Son of Man", which showed Him to be a man divinely ordained to bring to Israel the ideal rule of Yahweh Himself.

What do these three themes tell us? God had formed a community to which He had committed Himself in a loving covenant. For their part, the Chosen People were to live in such a manner as to illustrate the fact that God rules their lives. To live in this way and to inaugurate the Kingdom of God effectively, Yahweh would send His anointed one, the Messiah. Covenant, Kingdom of God, Messiah: here are three intertwining threads that are woven into the entire fabric of the Old Testament and highlight the central truth—that God loves His people and wants them to love Him in return. Just how far God would go in His love affair with man is categorically demonstrated in the New Testament.

The Gospels (CCC 125–27)

In the same way that the Old Testament was written to present theology and not history, so the Gospels were composed as theological reflections on the person of Jesus; they are not, strictly speaking, biographies of Jesus, nor were they intended for that purpose. The word "gospel" means "good news", and the good news the four evangelists wished to convey was that Jesus was the Messiah, the Son of God, the Savior of mankind. Because they wrote to different people at different times, their approaches were different.

Do differences lessen the credibility of the Gospels? Not at all. The central truths are all there. Each Gospel writer had been intrigued by a certain aspect of the personality of Jesus and accented it because he felt that his readers would best understand that particular picture of Jesus. Although the analogy limps, an example may be helpful. If someone wants a reproduction of the likeness of a loved one, he may seek out a portrait artist or a photographer. Both reproductions would be true, but each one would highlight a different aspect of the subject according to the method proper to the medium used. The situation with the Gospels is quite similar.

How were the Gospels written? For many years after the death and Resurrection of Christ, nothing was written about His life and teachings, and oral tradition (handing down of information by word of mouth) was extremely important (CCC 126.2). Certain key sayings of Jesus were remembered and carefully retained. Some Scripture scholars believe they were even written down (CCC 126.3). Mark then wrote his Gospel, upon which Matthew and Luke relied heavily, adding their own material and insights as well. Because of the similarities in content among these three Gospels, they are often referred to as the "Synoptic Gospels".

Why was information about Jesus passed on orally for so long? First of all, we must recall that writing materials were not as easy to obtain then as they are today. Second, the Church was just beginning; it was a long and gradual process before believers grasped the full impact of Jesus and their own identity. Third, we should remember that Christianity was unpopular and persecuted in many quarters; it was an "underground" religion that could not safely commit very much to writing.

Modern man may become alarmed at a prolonged period of oral tradition because of fears that something might have been lost or distorted. These fears can be dispelled by two considerations: religious and sociological. I mentioned earlier that Scripture was inspired and, as such, has God's guarantee of credibility. Therefore, the whole process of revelation is protected: oral and written. Second, it is well known that Orientals (Near East as well as Far East), especially in ancient times, possessed exceptionally keen memories. Although God chose fallible humans as His instruments of revelation, He can, as the maxim reminds us, write straight with crooked lines.

Once the evangelists began to write, their approach was

very different from that of modern biographers. They were intent on presenting the core of the Christian message, which revolves around the paschal mystery of Christ's Passion, death, and Resurrection. They started there and worked backward into events from the public ministry of Jesus and, only lastly, into accounts of His infancy. While these other events were of interest, they were of secondary concern. What gave meaning to these secondary concerns was the primary core doctrine: that Jesus suffered, died, and rose again. In other words, it would have made little difference if on a given day a certain man named Jesus expelled people from the Temple were it not for the fact that this Jesus was a unique individual, as demonstrated by the events of Holy Week.

With some of the preliminary groundwork completed, we can now come to the Gospels with a deeper appreciation and thus obtain a more profound meaning.

The Jesus of the Gospels

Scholars generally agree that Mark's was the first Gospel written, probably about thirty-five years after the Resurrection of Jesus. A more ancient opinion—and one regaining respectability and currency—is that an Aramaic version of Matthew's Gospel was first, having been committed to writing within a decade of the Lord's death and Resurrection. The general theme and organizing principle of Mark's Gospel may be seen as "triumph through suffering". In so many ways, Mark makes a point of bringing to the fore many of Jesus' sayings on suffering as it relates to His disciples and Himself. Why was Mark so careful in selecting such sayings? It appears that he was writing his Gospel for a persecuted Christian community in Rome. Mark saw this as an opportunity to strengthen these converts, to remind them that their Lord suffered but was ultimately victorious and that they could be, too—if they were faithful to Him. In this light, Mark's frequent allusions to the cross take on the most meaning.

While Mark's Christ is a suffering servant, He is still a person of immense authority. And it is this authority that must have appealed to that Roman audience. His manner of teaching (1:22) is unprecedented. He is able to put people in touch with the mystery of the Kingdom of God (4:11; CCC 546). He presents Himself as superior to the law (7:8–16; CCC 581), the Sabbath (2:28; CCC 2173), the Temple (11:15), and nature (4:41, 6:51). Finally, He has power over unclean spirits (3:23) and the power to forgive sins (2:5; CCC 1441). A careful reading of this Gospel will be most beneficial in discovering some of the very special theological treatments rendered by the other evangelists.

The Gospel of Matthew was written with the sayings of Jesus and, possibly, the Gospel of Mark as the source documents. Matthew was directing his message to Jewish converts, and he stressed the fact that conversion to Jesus does not mean entrance into a new religion but rather the only logical perfection of Judaism. The frequency of citations from the Hebrew Scriptures is a constant reminder of this, as Matthew uses the Scriptures to show how Jesus is truly the long-awaited Messiah.

The picture of Jesus we get from Matthew is a thoroughly Jewish one. He quotes the Old Testament prophets extensively, is familiar with Jewish customs, and parallels the experience of Israel in many ways, especially as we see Jesus in the flight into Egypt and His temptations. The Jesus of Matthew is a real "son of David". Jesus promulgates His New Law, like Moses, from a mountain (5:1ff.; CCC 581). And so, Matthew presents Jesus teaching His New Law (the Gospel) to the New

Israel (the Church); in Him the Old Law attains perfection and reaches its fulfillment.

An important theme in this Gospel is the Kingdom of Heaven. Mark and Luke refer to it as the Kingdom of God, but Matthew's wording points to the same reality. (Matthew substitutes "Heaven" for "God" because of the Hebrew tendency to avoid using the name of God.) The Kingdom is inaugurated with the preaching of Jesus, and His signs of healing give credibility to His claim that the reign of God has begun. However, this Kingdom of Heaven is not yet here in full force; it is the task of the Church to hasten its coming (Mt 16:16ff.; CCC 2818) and to pray for its arrival in power and glory (6:10). The thirteenth chapter of Matthew is devoted to a description of the characteristics of the Kingdom through the use of the famous parables of the seed, the weeds and wheat, the mustard seed, the hidden treasure, the net. Thus, Matthew presents his audience with the twofold aspect of the mystery: Jesus has established the Kingdom of Heaven, but its full realization is contingent upon the Church's work to "make disciples of all nations" (28:19; CCC 1122). Matthew sets the Church's agenda for all ages.

Luke's Gospel has been characterized as the "Gospel of the Spirit". Mary conceives through the overshadowing of the Spirit (1:35; CCC 437, esp. 484): Jesus launches His public ministry "in the power of the Spirit" (4:14); it is the same Spirit Who guides the Church in her life, in what some scholars consider the second half of Luke's Gospel, the Acts of the Apostles.

Luke has a universalistic dimension to his Gospel; he points out how the message of Jesus is for all, regardless of national, economic, or social background; unlike Matthew's, Luke's genealogy is not limited to Jesus' Jewish background, but He is placed right in the entire human family, all the way back to

Adam (3:23–38); at the Child's birth we meet shepherds (2:8); as He is presented in the Temple, He is proclaimed "a revealing light to the Gentiles" (2:32); He associates "with tax-collectors and non-observers of the law" (5:30).

Luke's Jesus is a model of prayer. He teaches His disciples a prayer (11:24) and encourages perseverance as well as trust in God's providential care (11:5–13; CCC 2613). He offers praise to His Father for blessing the disciples' endeavors (10:21f.) to make known His message. From the Cross, He asks the Father's forgiveness of His executioners (23:24; CCC 597) and places His life in His Father's hands (23:46; CCC 730).

Luke accents the compassion of Jesus, Who is merciful to sinners (7:48; CCC 1441) and to those who return (ch. 15). The thrust of Jesus' teaching is contained in 6:17–49, where He enjoins regard for the lowly, mercy, love, forgiveness, integrity, and fidelity upon His disciples. Jesus expects His followers to do likewise. Therefore, Luke's Gospel has a strong social message.

Luke is a very sensitive author and stresses this aspect of Jesus' personality as well. Luke's Jesus impresses us as very tender, perhaps because Luke so often places Him in the company of women (7:11, 7:37, 8:1, 8:43, 10:38, 13:11, 21:1, 23:27) and children (8:54, 18:16). However, there is also a theological reason for the predominance of women and children, and it takes us back to a theme discussed earlier. Luke wished to demonstrate very graphically that no one was to be excluded from the Church because of sex, intelligence, or social status.

Finally, Luke sees the work of Jesus as being continued in the Church. In fact, there is no difference between the ministry of Jesus and the ministry of the Church. One post-resurrectional event highlights this point: when the disciples meet the man on the road to Emmaus (24:13ff.; CCC 1347), they do not recognize Him; once He reenacts the "breaking of the bread", they know it is Jesus; at that moment, He disappears. Luke is trying to tell His early Church that to have the eucharistic Jesus is just as beneficial as experiencing His presence when He walked the roads of Galilee. Why? Because Jesus lives in His Church through the Spirit He sent. For Luke, no more is necessary.

The Gospel of John is so theological that justice can never be done to it merely in summary form. Because of the complexity of this Gospel, many scholars now believe that this work was composed over many years and went through many editions to reach its current perfection of literary style and theological sophistication.

A few basic considerations would be of use as a prelude to further study. At one time it was thought that John's Gospel was permeated with Greek philosophy, but we now see that it is also so Jewish that the allusions made are subtle and not explicit. Many aspects of the structure, language, and symbolism of this Gospel provide us with much of John's insight into Who Jesus was and is.

In the prologue (1:1–18), John begins with a hymn of praise to Jesus, God's Word, Who makes God present among us; He shows us what God is like (CCC 291). The body of the Gospel can be divided into the Book of Signs and the Book of Glory.

This Gospel emphasizes the work of Jesus as bringing about a "new creation". The Gospel is so structured that the author has Jesus work seven "signs" (a "sign" indicates the inbreak of the Kingdom of God) of mounting interest and importance. The signs are the "work" of God; Jesus is to do His Father's work. At Cana, water is changed to wine. A Jew, understanding his Scriptures, would immediately recall that bounty and plenty were signs of the Kingdom. In fact, the wedding feast itself served as a reminder of the marriage of God to His people (Hos 2:21ff.). He cures an official's son and a sick man; He feeds a large multitude from a few loaves and fishes; He walks on the sea; He cures a man born blind. Jesus' sign-working reaches a crescendo when He raises Lazarus from the dead, for "then you shall know that I am the LORD, when I open your graves and have you rise from them" (Ezek 37:13). This act becomes a fitting prelude to His own Resurrection.

Jesus works His signs so that, having seen the power of God, all might believe that He has been sent by God. Seeing leads to believing. Jesus also reveals His "glory". The Hebrew word for "glory" indicates a revelation of the divine presence. Thus, the evangelist again and again reverts to his thesis regarding Jesus: "Whoever has seen me has seen the Father" (Jn 14:9; CCC 470).

Another interesting note is the many times Jesus uses the phrase "I Am" in this Gospel. The reader will recall that "I Am Who Am" was the divine name revealed to Moses (CCC 205–7). The Gospel of John brings out this identification of Jesus and His Father by using this expression often (see 8:23–24, 8:28, 8:58).

The Book of Glory begins with the Last Supper. Jesus' hour of glory begins here, as He accepts His Father's will for Him, instructs His disciples, and prays for them. Chapters 14 through 17 present the Lord's farewell address. It is an exhortation to love, a warning of the world's hate, the promise of the Spirit and the return of Jesus, a prayer for the unity of the flock and for all who will ever believe in Him. We encounter a very moving discourse, all placed within the context of the Last Supper. John omits the accounts of the institution of the Eucharist because he has already dealt with this topic (6:54) and because the sacrificial love that prompts Jesus to wash the feet of His disciples is the same love that prompted Him to give them His promise of the Eucharist. John's concern is that the disciples learn to act like people who possess the gift of the Lord's presence by their attitudes of love, service, and unity.

John is also very interested in making some key sacramental allusions. The wine of Cana has eucharistic overtones, as does the discourse on the bread of life (6:25ff.). From the Lord's wounded side flow blood and water (19:34), which should remind Christians of their initiation into the community of faith through baptism and the Eucharist. Like Luke, John wishes to show the continued presence of Christ in His Church (CCC 1225).

Some people have labeled this Gospel "anti-Semitic", but this is to misinterpret John's language. When John speaks of "the Jews" in a derogatory manner, he refers to faithless Jews or the authorities responsible for the death of Jesus. On the other hand, faith and integrity are seen as characteristic of a "true Israelite" (1:47). The hostility, then, is not directed toward a race of people but toward a refusal to believe.

Because of Jesus' signs, people are expected to believe. Jesus' signs are His credentials, His proof. There is extensive use of legal terminology in the Gospel of John: witness, testimony, truth, advocate, judgment, accuser, evidence, condemnation, convict. In spite of all the evidence of the works of God that Jesus performs, "the world" (= unbelievers) still does not accept Him. And this is their condemnation.

The Goal of the Gospels

All of the Gospels were written as documents of faith. Each Gospel-writer wanted to put his readers in touch with Jesus so that they might attain salvation (see CCC 1846). The Gospels inform us of the works of Jesus and His preaching. His life makes demands on our lives. If we respond with faith, then the saying of the risen Lord to Thomas was said with us in mind: "Blessed are those who have not seen and have believed" (Jn 20:29).

Life in the Early Church

As a matter of fact, many did believe, and these people formed the primitive Church, about whom Luke writes in his Acts of the Apostles and to whom Paul and other disciples directed that body of New Testament literature called "epistles".

These works should be read not simply as history but as God's message to you at this particular moment. The reader should not look for a completely refined understanding of the identity of Jesus or the Church, nor should one expect a coherent and systematic exposition of Christian doctrine. That would be to make unrealistic demands on the early Church. It would also be well to observe closely the dedication, faith, and love of the early Christians as they witnessed to Jesus by their preaching of His message and by their living as His community, His people.

It would be impossible to consider each of the remaining books of the New Testament in the proper detail. Rather our intention is simply to summarize some main lines of thought. There is no substitute for personal reading and reflection.

The Acts of the Apostles

Luke composed the Acts of the Apostles as a companion volume to his Gospel. It is the story of the spread of Christianity to various parts of the world through the efforts of the apostles, especially Peter and Paul. One of the main difficulties facing the early Church was that of Gentile converts. The mission to the Jews was failing, while the preaching to the Gentiles had relative success. The question arose: "Are these Gentile converts bound to the Mosaic law?" At the "Council of Jerusalem" the matter was presented for consideration and discussion. The answer came: "It is the decision of the Holy Spirit and of us not to place on you any burden beyond these necessities, namely, to abstain from meat sacrificed to idols, from blood, from meats of strangled animals, and from unlawful marriage. If you keep free of these, you will be doing what is right" (Acts 15:28f.). Thus, the argument of those who wished to impose circumcision and other Jewish practices on Gentile converts was defeated. The point was made that faith in Jesus Christ was sufficient, a point to be emphasized and developed by Paul in two of his epistles.

The key concept in that apostolic letter was that the decision was made in accordance with the intention of the Holy Spirit.

In other words, the apostolic Church identified her actions with those of the Holy Spirit. For them, the Spirit Who was in Jesus was now given to them. In fact, this event is so important to Luke that he treats it in a unique and dramatic manner: the Spirit descends on the apostles (see Acts 2:3) as He descended on Jesus (see Lk 3:22). And the Church ever since has believed and preached the consoling doctrine of the indwelling of the Spirit, Who gives us courage and keeps us faithful to the Lord (CCC 797–98).

The Pauline Letters

The epistles of Paul were, in many ways, the first theological handbooks of the early Church. In them, Paul instructs his converts in Christian doctrine and urges them to live up to the high standards of Christian morality. They were very practical letters, written to reply to real-life situations and problems. We shall try to consider them in their chronological order rather than in their order of appearance in the New Testament.

The first letters were to the Christian community at Thessalonika, around A.D. 50–51. These two letters involve two closely connected topics: death and the Parousia (the Second Coming of Christ; CCC 673ff.). Many Thessalonians were reacting to the death of loved ones like those "who have no hope" (1 Th 4:13) in the resurrection of the dead. Paul asserts the constant teaching of Christ and His Church: death is not the end; the faithful are destined for life with God.

The Second Coming presented many difficulties for the first Christians because Jesus gave them no idea of when this would occur. At times He suggested that it would be relatively soon, while at others He said that He did not know Himself. Paul stresses the uncertainty of "the day of the Lord" and, therefore, the need for vigilance and preparedness. In his second letter, he cautions against an idleness whose excuse is that one is waiting for the Lord (2 Th 3:6f.). To this day, Christians have lived their lives by waiting "in joyful hope for the coming of our Savior, Jesus Christ".

Around A.D. 56–57, Paul wrote his two letters to the Corinthians: 1 Corinthians contains magnificent summaries of the Christian faith; 2 Corinthians is largely a defense of Paul's ministry to counteract the claims of his opponents. Paul's moral prescriptions to the Christians in this city of notoriety are firmly rooted in Christian beliefs. That is to say, Christians must act in a certain way because of the beliefs they profess. In his first letter Paul endeavored to reply to urgent problems facing that local Church: moral conduct (5:1–13, 6:12–20), marriage and virginity (7:1–40), liturgical gatherings (10:14–22, 11:17–34), charisms (ch. 13 and 14), and many other topics of concern to that community.

Paul's teaching on the resurrection of the dead is a theological masterpiece. In chapter 15, he makes the connection between the Resurrection of Jesus and our own resurrection: "If the dead are not raised, then Christ was not raised; and if Christ was not raised, your faith is worthless" (15:16–17; CCC 997). While many aspects of Paul's letters have limited value inasmuch as they were aimed at problems that no longer exist, his exposition of the doctrine of the resurrection retains its validity and relevance, for Paul had really caught on to the implications of dying and rising with Christ.

Another passage worthy of note in this epistle is that devoted to charisms, or special gifts given to various members of the community (ch. 12–14; CCC 799–801). Here, Paul recognizes the diversity of gifts and their legitimate value because they come from the Spirit. However, these gifts must never be for self-aggrandizement but need to be subordinated to the common good (CCC 951) and subject to the judgment of those in authority in the Church (CCC 801). In the midst of this discussion, Paul presents his beautiful hymn of love, in which he extols the unfailing character of love: "So faith, hope, love remain, these three; but the greatest of these is love" (13:13).

The Epistle to the Galatians was probably written around the year 48. The letter was occasioned by the activities of Jewish Christians who advocated the observance of the Mosaic law. To add credibility to their position, they discredited Paul as inferior to the other apostles. Paul responded with a defense of his mission, but he also produced a work whose thesis is that Christians are absolutely free from the law (CCC 1972). This was the prelude to his famous discussion of freedom and law in his Epistle to the Romans, some ten years later.

In that epistle, Paul further developed and refined his thought. The main lines of his thinking may be summarized in this way: before Christ, salvation came through observance of the law, but this requirement had the effect of showing man's inability to do what God required; with Jesus, however, justification occurs through faith in Him—our works do not merit salvation for us, only faith does (he cites Abraham as the example of living by faith); the first Adam brought condemnation to all, the second Adam (Christ) brought salvation; His death brings us life; if we still need the law, His death had no value (CCC 1992). Christ, then, is the focal point; our salvation rests on our willingness to put our faith in Him. At times this doctrine has been misinterpreted to mean that good works are not necessary, but that is not what Paul had in mind. We must perform good works to be active and involved Christians, but we will not look at works as winning salvation for us, only as opportunities for demonstrating what the love of Christ compels us to do (CCC 1993).

Paul seems to have had a deep affection for the Christians in Philippi. In his letter to them, he exhorts them to maintain their unity and fidelity. From a doctrinal standpoint, this letter is very important because of the hymn to Christ (2:6–11), in which Jesus is proclaimed as having preexisted with the Father but as not clinging to His divinity in becoming a man for our sakes. Because of his obedience in suffering, Jesus is exalted. Therefore, it is proper to acclaim Him as "Lord"; the Greek word *Kyrios* is used, which translates the Hebrew *Yahweh*. Thus, Jesus is presented as divine; this passage is probably the clearest New Testament statement of Jesus' divinity (CCC 446–51).

The Epistle to the Colossians stresses the primacy of

Christ, Whose place cannot be obfuscated by any other heavenly beings, for "all things were created through him and for him" (1:16; CCC 331). Through baptism, we are united to this sovereign Christ and are called upon to die to sin (3:5–10), in order to live a new life of virtue and love (3:12–16).

Once again, in the Epistle to the Ephesians, we hear about the cosmic significance of Christ, Who has given us "the first payment against the full redemption of a people God has made his own, to praise his glory" (1:14). Salvation has come to all through Christ's death, by which our sins were forgiven. Through that same death, men are reconciled to one another and united in the Church. Paul's understanding of the Church is discussed here; she is the instrument of salvation, the Body of Him Who is her head (see Eph 1:15–23; CCC 792). Because of their great dignity, Christians are called upon to live lives worthy of their calling (4:1). As usual, Paul ties in moral behavior with doctrinal tenets.

The Epistle to Philemon is more a postcard than a letter, but it does give us an insight into Paul's sensitivity as he pleads for kindness and mercy for a runaway slave.

The Epistles to Timothy and Titus have been characterized as the "Pastoral Letters" because of their concern about the preservation and transmission of sound doctrine and also the setting of criteria for ministry in the Church. These epistles provide the basis for a more structured approach to Christianity (rather different from that of the Church of Corinth), so that many scholars regard these letters as the foundation for "early Catholicism". Whether Paul or a disciple of his wrote these letters is a disputed question, but they are accepted as canonical and, therefore, inspired books.

The author of the Epistle to the Hebrews has been unknown from earliest times. Some have suggested Paul as the author; there are traces of Pauline theology, but there is no compelling evidence for this opinion. The letter is a beautiful appeal for perseverance in the Christian faith to people who are experiencing pressure from outside forces, as is the Book of Revelation (and so not intended as kind of a crystal ball for those infatuated with the end of the world). The author speaks of Jesus as God's last word (1:2; CCC 65) in a whole series of words throughout salvation history. He also shows how Jesus is the perfect high priest because of His sinlessness. He further demonstrates how the Old Testament and its sacrifices had value—but a limited value in view of the incalculable merit of Christ's sacrifice, for now everything finds its meaning and fulfillment in Him. This letter is important because it has strongly influenced the development of the Catholic theology of the priesthood and the Sacrifice of the Mass (CCC 1330).

The Catholic Epistles and Revelation

The letters of James, Peter, John, and Jude are called the "Catholic Epistles" because they are addressed to the whole Christian Church and not to particular individuals or communities.

The Epistle of James is a sermon exhorting Christians to good works, which is a further explanation and balancing out of Paul's teaching in Romans. This letter also warns against a vicious tongue, presumption, judgment of others, and riches. The author encourages patience and prayers for the sick (the basis for our sacrament of the sick [CCC 1510]).

The First Letter of Peter may stem from an early baptismal liturgy in which the newly baptized were given a strong christological foundation for the practice of virtue. It is an invaluable summary of apostolic theology and stresses the need for fortitude and perseverance despite trial and persecution. The Second Letter of Peter warns against false teachers and seeks to dismiss the fears of those who are anxious over the delay of the Parousia.

The three letters of John are involved with the themes of light, love, and truth. Faith in Jesus Christ must lead to love of our brothers: "Whoever says he is in the light, yet hates his brother, is still in the darkness" (1 Jn 2:9). The second letter is especially important because it emphasizes the fact that Jesus truly became a man (CCC 456ff.), written against those who had either denied or "spiritualized" the meaning of the Incarnation. The third letter is a plea to obey legitimate Church authority. The beauties of poetic style as well as the timeliness of their messages warrant a careful reading of these letters.

The Epistle of Jude denounces the false brethren who have infiltrated the Church, exaggerating Christian freedom and rejecting authority. Believers are then admonished to grow in faith and love through prayer and concern for their brothers and sisters.

One of the more puzzling books in Scripture is the Book of Revelation, with its symbolic, cryptic language in the tradition of Ezekiel, Zechariah, and Daniel. It was written to meet the crisis of the Roman persecution, and it encourages Christians to stand firm and avoid compromise. The Book of Revelation has an eschatological perspective in that it shows ultimate victory occurring at the end of time when Christ comes in glory, but it also teaches that the struggle is already over because Jesus has conquered Satan, sin, and death by His own redeeming death. The support provided by this book assisted the members of the early Church to be faithful witnesses to Christ and His message; their confidence has been passed down to successive generations, so that the faithful have suffered persecution confident of final vindication and glory. As with most prophetic works, the focus was on the present far more than on the future; hence, it reflects a poor understanding of biblical theology to attempt to find in Revelation detailed clues about life in the twentieth century, much less condemnations of contemporary individuals or groups.

The Scriptures in the Church

In addition to the personal reading of Scripture, the Church has two most important uses for these sacred writings: as a basis for doctrine and in the liturgy.

The Christian religion is a "book religion" inasmuch as the Bible is normative for Christian doctrine. No doctrine may ever be proposed for belief that contradicts an explicit teaching of Scripture, for, as Vatican II reminds us, the Church "has always regarded, and continues to regard, the Scriptures, together with sacred Tradition, as the supreme rule of faith. For since they are inspired by God and committed to writing once and for all time, they present God's own Word in an unalterable form, and they make the voice of the Holy Spirit sound again and again in the words of the prophets and apostles" (*Dei Verbum*, no. 21; CCC 80, 86, 108).

That does not mean we must limit ourselves to the statements of faith we find in the Bible; no, growth and development are needed. In fact, we see this process of increased understanding within the New Testament itself in regard to the Church's reflection on Jesus, His message, and the Church. Furthermore, refined concepts often come only after living a mystery for a period of time. Could we legitimately expect the apostles to have concluded immediately that Jesus was divine? That would be most unrealistic. No, it was after the passage of much time that we reached a very precise christological doctrine. In fact, it took nearly three hundred years to move from Paul's scriptural confession that "Jesus Christ is Lord" (Phil 2:11) to the Council of Nicaea's further explicitation of that insight in which we affirm that He is "true God from true God" (CCC 113).

The Scriptures take on a special depth of meaning when read in the context of the liturgy (CCC 127, 1100–1102). This is so because the Spirit Whom Jesus promised is there in a unique manner when Christians assemble to worship their Lord. The Church identifies herself with the Chosen People of the Old Testament and sees herself in continuity with the first Christian community described in the New Testament, as the God Who revealed Himself to Israel reveals Himself once more when we approach Him in faith and love. His Word challenges us and gives us confidence in our efforts to be faithful followers of Christ; that Word is enfleshed in the celebration of the Eucharist, to which we now turn our attention.

III

A Biblical Theology of the Mass

Even the least knowledgeable seem to know that the Mass is the central act of Catholic worship. Detractors of the Church often charge that the rites of the Mass are "man-made" and, on that score, idolatrous. The purpose of this chapter is to demonstrate the biblical basis for both the ritual and theology of the Mass, firmly situated in both Testaments and thus ever valid.

The Jewish Roots of the Liturgy

More than two decades ago, I taught in a parish school that stood directly opposite a Hebrew day school. At least once a year, children from both schools experienced each other's liturgy. As it happened, on one occasion I was unable to prepare the Jewish children for the Mass and feared they would be lost. Afterward, to my amazement and delight, I discovered that they had understood the liturgy as well as our own students—and perhaps even better. The Liturgy of the Word (CCC 1349), they said, was just like their own Sabbath service in the synagogue. The Offertory prayers (CCC 1350) sounded like their meal prayers. All the references to the "Lamb of God" and sacrifice reminded them of their Passover celebration (CCC 1362ff.). That incident convinced me that Pope Pius XI was right when he declared, "Spiritually, we are all Semites." In fact, this is so true that an inability to understand our Jewish roots has the effect of diminishing our grasp and appreciation of the Church's liturgical practice, which is largely an inheritance from Judaism (CCC 1096).

The Christian indebtedness to Judaism is strong and essential to acknowledge. In the early Church, Marcion attempted to "rid" the Church of Jewish remnants, including the Old Testament itself. The Church responded to Marcion's efforts by declaring him a heretic, launching the Church on a path to which she has remained faithful to this day (CCC 123). It is interesting to note that the scent of Jewish liturgical life is usually more easily detected in Catholicism than in Protestantism. Why so? Of course, the Reformers were intent on a "purified" and stripped-down liturgy, but another clear cause was often their own anti-Semitism (and this most definitely in the case of Martin Luther), which blinded them to the benefits of maintaining that historical link with Judaism.

If Christianity is to be in continuity with classical Judaism (and it should be, if we take seriously our Lord's words in Matthew 5:17 [CCC 592]), then that should be apparent in our doctrine (ethical monotheism) and in our liturgy. That relationship is depicted on one of the portals of Chartres Cathedral, as all the apostles stand on the shoulders of the prophets. How has this dependence been expressed liturgically?

We know from the Scriptures that Jesus was a devout and observant Jew: He engaged in private prayer, went to the synagogue faithfully, and participated in the Temple liturgies (CCC 583ff.). His early followers imitated His example, so that the first Church history textbook tells us that "they went to the temple area together every day, while in their homes they broke bread" (Acts 2:46). In other words, those early believers in Christ held on to their Jewish traditions and then added to them the specifically Christian "breaking of the bread" or Eucharist (CCC 1329). As time went on, authorities in Judaism, beleaguered from without by the Romans, came to the conclusion that the presence of these "Nazarenes" within their community was divisive and had to be eliminated. Hence, a nineteenth benediction (really a malediction) found its way into the synagogue liturgy, cursing the "sectarians" and effectively driving them out of institutional Judaism. Those Christians took with them the synagogue service and tacked it onto the breaking of the bread (replete with Passover symbols), so that the Mass throughout the ages (CCC 1345–46) has been a service in two parts: Liturgy of the Word and Liturgy of the Eucharist (CCC 1408). Ironically, early Christianity took in not only basic Pharisaic doctrines (like the resurrection of the dead) but also Pharisaic prayer forms, reflecting Christ's own predisposition to Pharisaism, even if He often disagreed with the Pharisees' style or methods of operation.

Synagogue worship, right up to the present, is a heavily verbal ritual: prayers, psalms, and Scripture readings. It also includes the primitive Jewish creed: "Hear, O Israel, the Lord our God is Lord alone. . . ." Blessings were also a part of the service.

The Scripture readings in our Lord's time were based on a three-year cycle, just as they are in contemporary Catholic liturgy. The Hebrew lectionary began on the Sabbath after the Feast of Tabernacles and ended on the last day of the same feast. It provided for a continuous reading from the Torah (first five books of the Bible) and also a passage from one of the prophets, used to explain the first reading or the particular feast. This is precisely the model for our selection of readings: the second reading is generally continuous from one of the epistles, while the Gospel reading and the first reading from the Hebrew Scriptures dovetail.

The Torah was brought to the *bima* (lectern or pulpit) in solemn procession, accompanied by the singing of psalms, and then the appropriate readings were chanted by a priest, levite, or scholar (in order of preference), especially if this occurred in the synagogue attached to the Temple. The congregation responded to the readings with the equivalent of our "Thanks be to God", and the sacred scroll was then returned to the ark.

Temple and synagogue liturgical forms also contributed significantly to the Christian celebration of the Liturgy of the Hours (CCC 1174, 1178). As we endeavor to determine the influence of these two institutions on the Church, some interesting facts come to the fore. First, in the historical playing out of events, not infrequently as certain elements of Jewish liturgy were appropriated by Christianity, they were subsequently abandoned by Judaism. Second, after the destruction of the Temple in A.D. 70, the synagogue shied away from Temple liturgical style (perhaps because of too painful a memory), while the Church with the passage of time increasingly drew on the Temple cult for her own worship, especially as the Jewish priesthood gradually died out and fear of confusion with it or its rites no longer existed.

Short congregational acclamations—such as "amen" ("Yes, it's true!" [CCC 1061–65, 2856, 2865]), "alleluia" ("Praise God!"), and "hosanna" ("God saves!")—and various doxologies (CCC 2855) or hymns of praise were important, particularly to facilitate the participation of illiterate people. In this context, it is worth noting that the liturgical services of both synagogue and Temple were conducted in Hebrew—by the time of Jesus, no longer a vernacular language but an exclusively sacral language, since the tongue spoken for daily affairs was Aramaic. Hence, Judaism's use of Hebrew can be seen as the precedent for the Church's use of Latin, even though Latin was a vernacular language when the Church first adopted it for her formal prayer life.

Besides the Scripture and Passover rites, the student of Christian liturgy can find other parallels to Jewish worship. Baptismal-like ceremonies and ritual baths were very popular in Judaism, both in the mainstream and among the Essene monks of Qumran near the Dead Sea. The connection between Jewish and Christian marriage celebrations is notably evident when one considers the Eastern Churches (CCC 1623), where bride and groom are arrayed in royal attire, a procession occurs, and a meal is shared—all symbols of the messianic feast of the end-times, of which marriage is a sign (CCC 1612).

The Roman Canon (Eucharistic Prayer I) reminds us very powerfully of the Jewish roots of Christian liturgy by bringing to mind the figures of Abel, Abraham, and Melchizedek (CCC 1350). As we seek to delve ever more deeply into the mysterious relationship between Judaism and the Church— all according to divine providence, we believe, with Saint Paul—we shall come to see and to value the insight of that anonymous artist of Chartres: the teaching and prayer of the apostles indeed rest on the shoulders of the prophets.

The Eucharistic Meal

At the midpoint of the Eucharistic Prayer, the priest invites the congregation to "proclaim the mystery of faith". Notice, he does not say *a* mystery of faith but *the* mystery (see CCC 1327), because the whole of salvation history is summed up and localized in the Passion, death, Resurrection, and Second Coming of Christ commemorated in the Eucharist. It is necessary, then, to examine this mystery in a manner that will best suit our finite minds. This will be an exercise in *fides quaerens intellectum* (faith seeking understanding), not knowledge for its own sake but a knowledge that leads to appreciation and love.

Therefore, the better to understand, we must separate into categories the aspects of the Eucharist that are simultaneously present to God, but which unfold in the celebration. The first element to be considered is the concept of a meal (CCC 1382–90), which underlies any eucharistic theology and which is immediately apparent to our senses. For what would any uninitiated person first perceive about the Eucharist but the actions of eating and drinking? Once these notions are in place, we may move on to other areas of interest and concern to frame a balanced and cohesive theology of this sacrament.

For a Jew, every meal is a sacred event, as it forges bonds among those who dine together (and so, our Latin-based word *companion*, which connotes "one with whom one shares bread") and between the participants in the meal and Almighty God, the source of the food and of every good thing. Throughout the Scriptures, we encounter the Lord providing for the physical sustenance of His people, whether with manna, quail, or water from the rock. Christians have always seen in these divine gifts a prefiguring of Jesus' offering of Himself to us as the Bread of Life (see Jn 6).

Each and every meal points to and is a sign (or "sacrament", to use the Christian terminology) of the messianic banquet according to the thinking of a devout Jew. Is it any surprise, then, that Jesus took full advantage of this rich meal tradition in order to grant to His Church the gift of salvation—which is to say, Himself (CCC 1373ff.)—until the end of time? Pierre Benoit, the great Scripture scholar, put it thus: "By this decisive act in which He entrusts to food the eternal value of His redemptive death, Jesus consummated and estab-lished for all ages this homage of Himself and of everything to God." And how did He do this? According to the Synoptic and Pauline traditions (see Mt 26:26–29; Mk 14:22–25; Lk 22:15–20; 1 Cor 11:23ff.), it was in taking bread and giving thanks to the Father, and in doing the same with a cup of wine—characteristically Jewish actions with a long and sig-nificant history.

Berakah is a theologically "loaded" word, conveying the notions of blessing and thanksgiving. In other words, the Jewish "grace" before meals is an act of praise and thanksgiv-ing to God for all the good He has given to the human race, but *equally* for the good He is *in Himself*. Matthew tells us that Jesus pronounced a "blessing" over the bread (26:26) and ut-tered words of "thanksgiving" over the cup (26:27); these words are interchangeable and synonymous, as other biblical texts reveal (CCC 1347).

At the beginning of any Jewish meal, one witnesses a ritual hand-washing (and so, its carry-over into Christian liturgy). The head of the family then prays over the first cup of wine: "Blessed be thou, Yahweh, our God, King of the universe, who givest us this fruit of the vine." Taking the bread, he prays in the same way, making the appropriate substitution, "who bringest forth bread from the earth". Prior to chanting a whole series of berakoth, he encourages his companions to enter into this solemn act of praise with him: "Let us give thanks to the Lord our God." Can any Catholic not hear these words of ancient Israel in our own Offertory prayers and introduction to the Eucharistic Prayer?

To this point, no mention has been made of the Passover supper, or seder, with good reason. First of all, the basic meaning of the Eucharist resides in its being a meal in general and not necessarily a Passover meal. Secondly, because of conflicting scriptural data, it is not clear whether our Lord's Last Supper was a seder. How so? The Synoptic Gospels and Paul certainly present the Last Supper as a Passover celebration (CCC 1338). John, however, does not, for he indicates that Jesus was being sentenced to death at the very hour when the priests were beginning to slaughter the Passover lambs in the Temple (see Jn 19:14). What is one to make of this discrepancy?

The Synoptic and Johannine traditions can be reconciled thus: Jesus, knowing that His death would coincide with the slaying of the paschal lambs and still desiring greatly to eat the final Passover with His disciples (see Lk 22:15), anticipated it by a day (CCC 1339). Is this not presuming a genuine sense of boldness on Christ's part? Yes, it is, but it is helpful to recall that He took similar liberties in regard to the observance of the Sabbath, declaring that "the Son of Man is lord even of the sabbath" (Mk 2:28).

Regardless of the precise date of the Last Supper, both Synoptic and Johannine passages maintain paschal overtones, and surely this was in the mind of Christ as He again showed Himself to be in continuity with Jewish life and thought by using Israel's past history of deliverance from slavery and death (as celebrated in the seder) to offer the pledge of the definitive deliverance of humanity, achieved in His death and Resurrection. This particular meal could symbolize that reality in a special manner (CCC 1340). At the same time, since the Lord's Supper was not exclusively tied in with the Passover, His disciples would be free to celebrate it with great frequency and not only once a year.

John's account of the Last Supper has no institution narrative. Strange—until one realizes that none was needed by the time that Gospel was completed, some seventy years after Christ's return to the Father. Instead, we are permitted to "eavesdrop" on Jesus' berakah, or high priestly prayer, in John 17. In many ways, it could have served as a model for future Eucharistic Prayers; the part of the *Didaché* that contains the earliest known Eucharistic Prayer does, in fact, bear a considerable resemblance to it in language and style.

Jewish thought regards God's Word as powerful, accomplishing its purposes, and so we read in the Psalter that "by the word of the Lord the heavens were made". Therefore, when Jesus says, "This is my body" and "This cup is the new covenant in my blood", we must take Him at His Word and see in these actions a transformation as real and exciting as the creation of the universe from chaos at the dawn of time, or His own Incarnation in the womb of the Virgin Mary. God, Who fed His people in the desert, now, in Christ, "entrusts to food the eternal value of His redemptive death". This food to be eaten (for, as the Germans say, "a man is what he eats"), however, has a unique significance, intimately united to the Lord's self-sacrifice. It is only in reflecting on Christ's *death*, then, that we learn the full meaning of how Jesus is our Bread of *Life* (CCC 1364).

The Eucharistic Sacrifice (CCC 1365–72)

The mystery of the Eucharist may be compared to a multi-faceted diamond that, to be appreciated in all its complex beauty, needs to be studied from many angles and in various conditions of light and shadow. One such facet is that of sacrifice, for Catholic theology has always insisted that the Eucharist must be regarded as more than a meal—and with good reason.

Saint Paul sets forth the rationale for the position: "For our paschal lamb, Christ, has been sacrificed. Therefore, let us celebrate the feast . . ." (1 Cor 5:7–8; CCC 1364). Cardinal

Lustiger of Paris, a Jew by birth, understands clearly the implications of this Pauline teaching: "The lamb of the feast was sacrificed in the Temple. Without this reference, the very Eucharist loses its meaning."[1] In other words, the Lamb consumed at the seder must be eaten with one eye fixed on His sacrifice. How did Jews at the dawn of the Christian era perceive ritual sacrifice? Which is to say: How did Jesus perceive His own self-immolation and its perpetuation in the Eucharist?

Sociologists of religion point to the presence of sacrifice in all religions. Judaism offered a sacrifice of praise and thanksgiving and a sacrifice in atonement for sins, both personal and communal. These sacrifices required both a sacred place (the Temple) and a sacred minister (a priest). These rites were performed daily in the Temple at Jerusalem by the priests who represented the community of Israel before God, having the effect of renewing the covenant between Almighty God and the Chosen People. It will be recalled that, to seal a Semitic covenant, a real victim (standing in vicariously for the offerers) was required (see Gen 15:7–18; Ex 24:5f.), with the victim's blood being sprinkled on the altar of sacrifice. Thus did the death (separation of body and blood) of the victim bring life (blood seen as the seat of life) to the beneficiaries of the rite. Peace offerings were also consumed by the participants.

The Passover meal contains numerous sacrificial and messianic allusions. The celebrant lifts up the bread and bitter herbs in a gesture of sacrifice; in the days of the Temple, the shankbone of the lamb was raised in offering. The cup for Elijah is a reminder of the constant hope for the coming of the Messiah, as the people pray that the Lord would "hasten

---

[1] Jean-Marie Cardinal Lustiger, *Dare to Believe* (New York: Crossroads, 1986), p. 82.

the day". The seder, therefore, looks to the past and the future simultaneously.

It is against this background of Jewish cult that one must regard the words and deeds of Jesus on Holy Thursday night. In the Synoptic accounts of the institution of the Eucharist (CCC 1323, 1337), Jesus indicates that the bread and wine presently being considered will attain their full significance at some future moment when the body "*will be* given up" and the blood "*will be* shed"—"for you", causing the apostles (and the Church ever since) to focus their gaze on Calvary because of the sacrificial language used. John's Gospel lets us hear Jesus describe the meaning of His actions through a lengthy discourse, reminiscent of the explanations written into the very text of the Passover rite. Furthermore, we acknowledge that the Eucharist is more than a meal because the Scriptures note that the origins of the Eucharist are not to be found exclusively in a meal, for we read that the *berakah* over the cup takes place *after* the supper (see Lk 22:20).

Our Lord also gives the definitive explanation of how all this is to be interpreted: ". . . Do this in memory of me" (Lk 22:19). The concept of memory is key to a genuinely Jewish (and biblical) understanding of the liturgy. The paschal meal, for instance, is not merely a passive, if fond, recollection of an occurrence of the distant past. Its present coming to memory makes it happen all over again, so that the meal's current celebrants are there in Egypt and participate in a real reenactment of that salvific event. Sacred memory leads to sacred reality. And so it is that Jesus wished His followers to regard the Eucharist in such a way that their ritual reenactment of the meal would bring to mind the salvation He won for all on the Cross and would likewise move them to look forward to the day of His return in glory (cf. the Elijah cup of the seder). By His instructing us to engage that most powerful of human faculties (memory) in such a way, the benefits of His redeeming death, offered once for all (see Rom 6:9), could be applied to us now. A proper understanding of the Eucharist, then, requires one to appreciate the fact that the Eucharist neither merely recalls nor actually repeats the once-for-all sacrifice of Christ, but renders it sacramentally (that is, really and truly) present (CCC 1363, 1364, 1085).

Very early on, the eucharistic words of Jesus became standardized or ritualized into liturgical formulations, enabling Paul in A.D. 56 to say: "I received from the Lord what I also *handed on* to you, that . . ." (1 Cor 11:23; italics mine). A liturgical tradition already existed. Many scholars believe that Luke 22:15–18 was originally a fragment of an old account of the Passover in which the paschal lamb is simply replaced by the offering of the Eucharist.

The four Eucharistic Prayers currently in general use throughout the universal Church all have ancient origins. Eucharistic Prayer I is a blending of the primitive Roman Canon and the Syrian tradition from Jerusalem; Prayer II is based on that of Hippolytus from the late second century; Prayers III and IV have their roots in the Apostolic Constitutions of the late fourth century. Throughout the history of the Church, it is important to observe, the liturgical prayers have always maintained the several elements of the Eucharist (meal, sacrifice, etc.) in a balanced juxtaposition. A good reminder of this is that the eucharistic bread is called a "host" from the Latin *hostia* (victim): thus, the Food that is received is the Victim Who has been offered.

One further note: sacrificial rites presume a priesthood. In the strictest sense, the covenant community of the New Dispensation knows only one priest—Jesus Christ (CCC 1544–45); any other priests function *in persona Christi* (CCC 1548). In the liturgy, the human priest weaves in and out of the community, so that at one moment he stands among the people and prays in the first person plural (for himself as much as for the congregation), while at other moments (the most significant) he stands at the head of the people—over against the congregation—taking on the voice of Christ: "This is *my* body." Similarly, "May Almighty God bless *you*", not *us*. No community or collective officiation at the Eucharist is possible (even in concelebration, one priest is designated *principal* celebrant) because, at the sign level, the headship and self-offering of Christ must be apparent (CCC 1368). Finally, the Christ Who offers Himself for the members of His Body, the Church, then feeds them. A unity of time is made, causing the worshipping community to gain a glimpse of eternity: the past sacrifice of Calvary makes us look to the future Parousia—all experienced as an ever-present "now" through the signs and symbols of the Eucharist.

The Passover table and the altar of the Cross are inseparably united. Holy Thursday's covenantal meal of promise is fulfilled in Good Friday's covenantal sacrifice. "For as often as you eat this bread and drink this cup, you proclaim the death of the Lord until he comes" (1 Cor 11:26). This sacrificial meal brings us into communion with Christ and one another, the point of the reflection that follows (CCC 1383).

Eucharistic Communion

One constant in sacramental terminology down the ages and across denominational lines seems to be the description of the act of eucharistic reception as "Holy Communion", and rightly so, for what else more aptly summarizes the meaning of the sacrament? The Roman Missal speaks of Holy Communion as "the sign and promise" of our unity in Christ (CCC 1391, 1402ff.). How is that so?

In both Hebrew and pagan worship, a clear connection was envisioned between the sacrifice offered and the symbolic meal following. Saint Paul reminded the Corinthians that just as the Jews of old were associated with the sacrificial rites by taking the sacrifice into themselves as food, so too do the pagans commune with the demons by participation in their rites. He warned the early Christians, therefore, not to involve themselves in pagan rituals but to restrict themselves to the eucharistic sacrifice and meal, for "The cup of blessing that we bless, is it not a participation [communion] in the blood of Christ? The bread that we break, is it not a participation in the body of Christ?" (1 Cor 10:16). But that's not all; the Eucharist has not only this vertical dimension of union between the believer and Christ but also a horizontal element—union among all who receive the sacrament. "Because the loaf of bread is one, we, though many, are one body, for we all partake of the one loaf" (v. 17; CCC 1396).

Communion with the Lord and with one another occurs as the sacrifice overflows into the meal: the Paschal Lamb is sacrificed for us (and for the whole of humanity) and then eaten, continuing the sacrifice within us, effecting our participation in it. It is no accident that the Lord's Prayer introduces the Communion Rite, whether that takes place within the Mass or outside it. That prayer, based on the eighteen Benedictions of the Jewish liturgy, admirably combines the vertical and horizontal concerns that should be uppermost in our minds as we endeavor to deepen our union with Christ and each other.

The careful reader will notice that I said "deepen" and not "cause". Receiving Holy Communion presupposes an existing relationship with Christ, caused by baptism and restored, if necessary, by sacramental penance (CCC 1385ff., 1415). Hence, Saint Paul cautioned the Corinthians against an unworthy reception of the Eucharist, which would bring on the reverse effects of that for which they hoped (see 1 Cor 11:22ff.). The Fathers of the Church often interpreted Jesus' parable of the wedding garment as the necessity of being in a state of baptismal innocence to approach the altar. It was surely this rationale that called for catechumens to leave the liturgical celebration before the Offertory (what we once knew as the Mass of the Catechumens, as distinct from the Mass of the Faithful). This understanding is still with us in two ways: the Church's insistence on one's being in a state of grace to receive Holy Communion and the Church's refusal to grant eucharistic Communion to non-Catholic Christians as a general rule (CCC 1398–1400).

This last point requires further explanation in these postconciliar days of heightened ecumenical awareness and activity.

While the Church will permit non-Catholics to receive Holy Communion from the hands of a Catholic priest under extraordinary circumstances (for example, where eucharistic belief is the same and yet one in danger of death or religious persecution does not have access to one's own minister), under similar circumstances Catholics may receive only from a validly ordained non-Catholic priest (for example, Eastern Orthodox), for reasons of eucharistic validity (CCC 1401).

The more general permission is denied, not to be mean-spirited, but as a reflection of our eucharistic theology, solidly grounded in the New Testament: Holy Communion is a sign of unity between a believer and Christ, yes, but equally a sign of unity among the believers themselves—ecclesial communion (CCC 1398). Where ecclesial communion does not exist in any substantive manner, the sacramental action is empty and meaningless at best and a lie at worst. Some people argue that intercommunion would bring about a unity deeper than what already exists among all Christian believers because of their common baptism, but that is an extremely minimalistic notion of Christian unity. Furthermore, the historical record demonstrates most convincingly and disappointingly that intercommunion among Protestants themselves has in no way made them closer to one another and has often allowed them to drift farther apart because of "sloppy" forms of ecumenism engendered by a too-hasty decision to enter into eucharistic communion without the prior basis of ecclesial communion.

Holy Communion is so important to us Catholics because we have taken to heart the insights of John 6, an early and comprehensive treatment on the significance of the Eucharist, especially in terms of its ability to keep us one with Christ and to lead us to everlasting life. Thus, the present union with the Lord is regarded as but a foretaste of that full union to be hoped for in heaven (CCC 1402, 1419). John the Evangelist is more emphatic than any other New Testament writer in asserting the necessity of the Eucharist for salvation (see 6:53), for he was dealing with Gnostics, a heretical sect that had allergic reactions to the visible or sensible signs of divinity, whether manifested in sacraments or an "institutional" Church, and claimed to have access to the Lord in "spiritual" ways, independent of the ecclesial Body of Christ. They were attempting to have Communion without communion. John's response to such a suggestion is a resounding No, for it pleased Christ to make Himself available to His Church through the outward signs of bread and wine, transformed through the faithful sacramental action of His Church. The union was to be real and tangible—body entering body.

What should be the results of a worthy reception of Holy Communion? First, a longing for heaven, where our experience of Christ will be direct and immediate, with no need for sacramental signs (CCC 1404). Second, an attitude of thanksgiving and thankfulness (the very meaning of Eucharist), which characterizes our whole life (CCC 1360). This desire is symbolized as the Church repeats the Opening Prayer of the Sunday Mass throughout the week in the Liturgy of the Hours: the continuation of the act of thanksgiving (Eucharist) in the prayer and work of every day. Third, participation in the works of charity as the individual believer recalls that the Lord Who died and rose for him expects him to be as selfless in his relations with others: "Love one another as I have loved you" (CCC 1394, 1397).

And thus we see ourselves come full-circle again with Communion in its vertical and horizontal dimensions.

Why do we go to Communion? Cardinal Lustiger says that "we go because Christ calls us, the Holy Spirit gathers us, and God commands us." In other words, the action of the Blessed Trinity in our lives leads us to Communion. It is the unfailing promise of Christ renewed in each Eucharist celebrated: "And when I am lifted up from earth, I will draw everyone to myself" (Jn 12:32). The grace of the Cross summons and draws us into unity, requiring a response of participation.

Ritual Elements of the Mass

"Man cannot live without adoring" (see CCC 28). This is one of my favorite quotes from Pope John Paul II, based as it is on solid psychology, sociology, philosophy, and theology and thus said by him with no fear of contradiction. By this assertion, the Holy Father means that every human being attains fulfillment in the act of worship, which orients a person toward the Ultimate. For that to be a truly human act, it must necessarily incorporate the entirety of the human person—body and soul alike. Hence, the concern with ritual in every age, culture, and religion, so ably expounded by someone like Mircea Eliade.

As an incarnational religion, Christianity has never hesitated to use created things to point toward the Uncreated One. The Church received a rich inheritance of liturgical ritual from her mother, Judaism. A careful examination of these elements will demonstrate both the continuity and catholicity of the Church down the ages, as we have been taught by the great liturgists of an earlier generation: Joseph Jungmann, Gregory Dix, Odo Casel.

Sociologists of religion regard ritual as a special divine language, communicating more through signs and symbols than through words. Jean Cardinal Lustiger again warns, in this regard, that "unless we learn the language of God [ritual], we risk remaining completely inarticulate." In other words, as body–soul entities, we receive from ritual the tools to speak to God and at the same time the tools to understand God (CCC 1145–52).

Being taken on a tour of the Temple in our Lord's day, an observer would be told that it housed the altar of sacrifice. The visitor would see candles flickering and smell incense burning. Someone might at that moment be reading from the Sacred Scriptures at the lectern. The scene appears no different from that in a contemporary Catholic church anywhere in the world (CCC 1154).

The very postures of prayer have always been important. The Psalter often indicates the various liturgical gestures and suggests their meaning. Kneeling and genuflection are signs of adoration. Folded hands bespeak subordination to the divine will. Prostration (still used with such powerful effect in our ordination liturgy) declares one's vulnerability as a believer and, hence, one's total dependence upon God. Raised or lifted hands beckon to the Almighty in petition.

Candles were used in Jewish prayer with special significance in both the Sabbath meal and the rites of the Temple and synagogue. They stood for joy (to greet the Sabbath) and for sorrow (and so were placed at the head of the deceased). For us Christians, candles symbolize Christ, the light of the world, as we proclaim dramatically in the Easter Vigil service.

Incense is a symbol that makes a strong appeal to the senses of sight and smell. "Let my prayer come like incense before you", prayed the inspired Psalmist (141:2). The sweet odor reminds worshippers of the loveliness of the heavenly Kingdom, of which they obtain but a glimpse in the earthly liturgy. The ancient Hebrew liturgy restricted incense to the Temple because of the unique presence of God in that especially sacred place. Normally, the high priest incensed the altar directly in front of the Holy of Holies, but on Yom Kippur, he ventured straight into the most sacred locus of divinity and there offered incense to the Almighty. Interestingly, in the Christian appropriation of this symbol, not only is the Divinity Himself so honored (for example, in the Blessed Sacrament) but also persons (made in the image and likeness of God) and things to be used in worship. Such an approach reflects the depths of Christian incarnational theology, so that all creation is considered worthy of veneration as manifestations of the divine in the world, created through and redeemed by Christ (CCC 2415).

While the Israelites believed their entire nation was a priestly people, they also acknowledged the need to set apart certain men to reflect that holiness of God in a special way and thus lead the whole people into that holiness—the very essence of priestly activity. These priests were to dress in a particular manner, especially for the offering of sacrifice (see Lev 8). Some of these vestments are still in use in the Church.

The alb (common to all sacred ministers) and the miter (the ceremonial headdress of the bishop) stand out as the best examples (see Ex 28). We know that many of our liturgical vestments were adapted from regular Roman street clothing; however, we also know that in the Middle Ages many liturgists made a conscious effort to reincorporate Jewish liturgical traditions into our own.

Whenever we begin Sunday Mass with the Asperges rite, we are harking back to the experience of Israel in Egypt (see Ex 12:22) and making our own the ancient Hebrew desire for forgiveness: "Cleanse me of sin with hyssop, that I may be purified" (Ps 51:9).

The Offertory procession (CCC 1350), restored to the liturgy in the postconciliar reform, was first introduced into Christian worship by Pope Gregory VII in the eleventh century. However, its origins may be found in the Temple cult. In Exodus 23 we hear the Israelites being encouraged to bring their gifts for sacrifice to the altar in solemn procession.

The imposition of hands is a venerable biblical gesture of acceptance and empowerment, so that it accompanied the reception of the gifts for sacrifice as well as the ordination of men to the priesthood. The high priest also imposed hands on the scapegoat of Yom Kippur as he symbolically unloaded the sins of the people onto the animal (see Lev 16:21). The imposition of hands is found in major Christian rituals to the present: the invocation of the Holy Spirit to transform the bread and wine of the Eucharist (CCC 1353); priestly ordination (CCC 1538); in the sacraments of confirmation (CCC 1288) and penance; solemn blessings.

Fasting as atonement for sins had an important place in biblical Judaism, but another kind of fasting was extremely crucial, namely, the requirement that the Passover supper be eaten on an empty stomach. How logical appear our own regulations on eucharistic fasting when seen in the light of Hebrew tradition.

Both instrumental and vocal music were highly regarded in the worship of synagogue and Temple. Antiphonal or responsive singing was the norm, as it made possible congregational participation in pre–printing-press days or in days of widespread illiteracy (CCC 1156–58). Readings from the Scriptures were chanted, as were the psalms. Hebrew chant, like Gregorian after it, had as its guiding principle the notion that the music should always serve the text, not the other way around.

All the sights and sounds of Hebrew liturgy coalesced to remind worshippers of the absolutely other and transcendent God Whom they loved and adored. It is, therefore, no surprise that so many important revelations (for example, the call of Isaiah in the Old Testament and the announcement to Zechariah in the New Testament) were made known in the course of a Temple service; the sense of awe and mystery disposed one to be attentive to divine promptings. And so we read: "I saw the Lord seated on a high and lofty throne with the train of his garment filling the temple. Seraphim were stationed above. . . . 'Holy, holy, holy is the Lord of hosts!' they cried one to the other. 'All the earth is filled with his glory!' At the sound of that cry, the frame of the door shook and the house was filled with smoke" (Is 6:1–4).

That experience of worship led Isaiah to discern his call. The Church's hope is that our experience of inspiring liturgy presented to our senses will make a claim on our minds and hearts. Hearing the Lord ask, "Whom shall I send? Who will go for us?" the Christian worshipper, similarly affected by the sacred rites, will echo the openness and enthusiasm of Isaiah: "Here I am; send me" (6:8). Liturgy, then, takes the things of this world, translates them into the language of divinity, and sends us forth to serve the Lord in serving others.

The Liturgical Cycle

Time is a most precious commodity, especially in these days of high mobility and hyperactivity. The person who has time or who makes time for others is truly in demand. Time, then, may be a trap or a gift. In its realism, the Judeo-Christian Tradition offers people the means to ensure the latter, and that is done through living human time according to the divine clock through a liturgical cycle that brings about the experience of eternity (an ever-present now) in the here-and-now. The whole purpose of referring to a liturgical "cycle" is precisely to point toward a never-ending, ever-repeating circle of time—eternity.

The first generations of Christians, as should now be clear, inherited and accepted a fully developed liturgy from Judaism, including its understanding of sacred time (CCC 1164). This is seen even in our regarding a liturgical day as beginning at sundown of the previous day (the explanation, by the way, for why a Saturday evening Mass can fulfill the Sunday obligation).

The central liturgical celebration for early Christianity was the commemoration of the Lord's Resurrection, observed not only on Easter, however, but on every Sunday. The seven-day week is not a division of time based on nature (like the day, the month, or the year) but one rooted in Genesis revelation describing the Almighty as resting on the seventh day, providing the Chosen People with a model for their own existence. In the subsequent Jewish reflection on this concept, the rabbis presented the Sabbath as a celebration of creation and an eschatological foretaste of the coming Kingdom.

No surprise, then, that the early Church could see the same theology aptly applied to the Resurrection, and hence the switch to Sunday (CCC 1166–67). Like their Jewish ancestors, Christians perceived the Sabbath as a day of joy unsuited to fasting or other penitential practices (CCC 2185). That is the reason, of course, why Sundays are not calculated in the reckoning of the Lenten season and why it is really incorrect to speak of a particular Sunday *of* Lent (instead of a Sunday *in* Lent).

From the Sunday celebration of the Lord's paschal mystery, the Church came to see the importance of extending that event to the entire week. This extension was made by adopting the synagogue service of morning and evening prayer and connecting them with the Sunday Eucharist—as is still evident in the repetition of the Opening Prayer of the Sunday Mass in the daily Liturgy of the Hours. Only later did daily Mass become commonplace, but again, the Opening Prayer on weekdays was often (and still is) the prayer of the preceding Sunday.

As the split between Judaism and Christianity became apparently irreversible, the Church gradually and consciously took over significant aspects of the various Jewish feasts (CCC 1096). Thus, the spring festivals of Passover and Pentecost came into the Church wholesale as the Easter–Pentecost observance of fifty days, for how appropriate that the memorial of the slaying of the paschal lamb should be transferred to the Paschal Lamb par excellence and that the recollection of the giving of the law should be translated into the birth of the Church, now Christ's special means of salvation for all.

The autumn feasts of Rosh Hashanah (New Year's Day) and Yom Kippur (Day of Atonement) came into Christian liturgy as the season of Advent, originally a period of six weeks for the "six Sabbaths of preparation" (CCC 1095).

Saint Jerome saw in Advent the same renewal theme found in Judaism, with the penitential emphasis and readings from Isaiah common to Judaism and Christianity. The relationship between the feast of the Epiphany and the feast of Succoth, with its stress on water and light, is especially clear in the Eastern rites, where both symbols are still given significant play.

The Sabbath is *so* key to Jewish life that years as well as days were looked upon from this perspective. So it is that seven Sabbaths of years were celebrated as a Jewish year of freedom and joy—the obvious origin of our own "holy years" (at the outset, every fifty years too, but now every twenty-five years).

Ancient Judaism also had a unique reverence for martyrs. Interestingly enough, the first feast days noted in the Christian calendar were those of martyrs, with the eucharistic sacrifice actually offered on the tomb of the saint (a remnant of which practice continues in the use of an altar stone). Gradually, other saints' feasts were added and were seen as both a continuation of the Lord's Passion and death in the lives of His faithful people and the victory of His Resurrection in them.

Human nature seems to have a basic desire to share in the experience of others, especially of one's beloved. This instinct surfaced in Christian worship as the liturgical cycle eventually "played out" the life of Christ, from His birth to His Resurrection and Ascension, to His sending of the Spirit and the formation of the Church, who looks forward to His glorious Second Coming. And so it is that each member of Christ's Body enters into the experience of the Head. As the Ascension Preface phrases it, "where He has gone, we hope to follow".

Participation in a sacral calendar is an important way of sanctifying the secular year, particularly in a post-Christian society (CCC 1168–71). It reminds all that at least some people march to the beat of a different drummer. Therefore, attending Sunday Mass and most especially observing the holy days of obligation (because this is so countercultural) can be seen as powerful acts of Christian witness in a civilization going or gone pagan.

Pausing to pray each day and especially on the Lord's Day is an acknowledgment of our origins and destiny in God; it is "touching base" with Reality and an implicit statement of one's desire to enter fully into that Reality at some future moment.

It is the sure conviction of Christian faith that time well spent is not only a preparation for eternity but a genuine if shadowy experience of it, as we are taken out of time and proleptically thrown into eternity. Through the liturgical cycle, the Christ Who redeemed mankind now redeems mankind's dearest possession—time.

Concluding Thoughts

Catholic theology subscribes to the principle of *lex orandi, lex credendi*, whereby one can determine Catholic doctrine by observing the Church's liturgy, because what we believe is enshrined in our worship (CCC 1124, 1327).

This chapter has been by no means an exhaustive survey of the biblical underpinnings for the Mass, yet even so one finds a bedrock of biblical theology, powerfully conveyed in sign and symbol. The same is found to be true when one examines the very words of the liturgy.

IV

Mass Prayers; Biblical Prayers

Chapter III asserted that the theology of the Mass is a biblically oriented prayer. However, it is not only the general theological thrust that is scriptural but even the very words themselves. The contents of this chapter will demonstrate that point. For the liturgical texts quoted here, I have given also the scriptural texts on which the liturgical prayers are based. Thus will become evident the degree to which theology and biblical text combine to form a thoroughly biblical form of prayer.

THE ORDER OF MASS

Introductory Rites

Priest: In the name of the Father, and of the Son, and of the Holy Spirit. —CCC 234

... baptizing them in the name of the Father, and of the Son, and of the Holy Spirit (Mt 28:19).

I wish to note here the research contributions of some former undergraduate theology students of mine at St. John's University: Brother Charles Brunner, S.S.P., Mrs. Dorothy MacIver, Mrs. Edna Fama, and Mr. Joseph Hickey.

People: Amen.

Let all the people say, Amen! (1 Chron 16:36).

The priest expresses the presence of the Lord to the community.

[A]

Priest: The grace of our Lord Jesus Christ and the love of God and the fellowship of the Holy Spirit be with you all.

—CCC 249

People: And also with you.

The grace of the Lord Jesus Christ and the love of God and the fellowship of the Holy Spirit be with all of you (2 Cor 13:13).

[B]

Priest: The grace and peace of God our Father and the Lord Jesus Christ be with you.

People: And also with you.

or

Blessed be God, the Father of our Lord Jesus Christ.

—CCC 2627

Blessed be the God and Father of our Lord Jesus Christ (1 Pet 1:3).

[C]

Priest: The Lord be with you.

People: And also with you.

The LORD be with you! (Ruth 2:4).

PENITENTIAL RITE

All: I confess to almighty God, and to you, my brothers and sisters, that I have sinned through my own fault

Therefore, confess your sins to one another and pray for one another, that you may be healed (James 5:16).

in my thoughts and in my words,

... do not be haughty... wise in your own estimation (Rom 12:16).

The tongue . . . exists among our members as a world of malice, defiling the whole body (James 3:6).

in what I have done, and in what I have failed to do;

So for one who knows the right thing to do and does not do it, it is a sin (James 4:17).

and I ask Blessed Mary [CCC 2618, 2677], ever virgin, all the angels and saints, and you, my brothers and sisters, to pray for me to the Lord our God.   —CCC 2634–36

Brothers, pray for us [too] (1 Th 5:25).

Priest: May almighty God have mercy on us, forgive us our sins, and bring us to everlasting life.

If we acknowledge our sins, he is faithful and just and will forgive our sins and cleanse us from every wrongdoing (1 Jn 1:9).

—CCC 1847

People: Amen (1 Chron 16:36).

All: Lord, have mercy.

Let us pray and beg our LORD to have mercy on us and to grant us deliverance (Tob 8:4).

All: Christ, have mercy.

. . . grace, mercy, and peace from God the Father and Christ Jesus our Lord (1 Tim 1:2).

Priest: Lord, we have sinned against you . . .   —CCC 1850

Against you only have I sinned, and done what is evil in your sight (Ps 51:6).

Priest: Lord, show us your mercy and love.

Do not let us be put to shame, but deal with us in your kindness and great mercy (Dan 3:42).

People: And grant us your salvation.

Show us, O LORD, your kindness, and grant us your salvation (Ps 85:8).

GLORIA

All: Glory to God in the highest, and peace to his people on earth.   —CCC 333

Glory to God in the highest / and on earth peace to those on whom his favor rests (Lk 2:14).

Lord God, heavenly King, almighty God and Father,

—CCC 865

Alleluia! The Lord has established his reign, [our] God, the almighty! (Rev 19:6).

we worship you,

Worship God (Rev 22:9).

we give you thanks,   —CCC 2742

. . . giving thanks always and in everything in the name of our Lord Jesus Christ to God the Father (Eph 5:20).

we praise you for your glory.   —CCC 2642

Amen! Blessing and glory, wisdom and thanksgiving, / honor, power and might / be to our God forever and ever. Amen! (Rev 7:12).

Lord Jesus Christ, only Son of the Father,   —CCC 444–45

Grace, mercy, and peace will be with us from God the Father and from Jesus Christ, the Father's Son in truth and love (2 Jn 3).

Lord God, Lamb of God, you take away the sin of the world: have mercy on us;   —CCC 523, 608

Behold the Lamb of God, who takes away the sin of the world (Jn 1:29).

you are seated at the right hand of the Father: receive our prayer.   —CCC 663–64

It is Christ [Jesus] who died, rather, was raised, who also is at the right hand of God, who indeed intercedes for us (Rom 8:34).

For you alone are the Holy One,

I know who you are—the Holy One of God! (Lk 4:34).

you alone are the Lord,

Who will not fear you, Lord, / or glorify your name? / For you alone are holy. All the nations will come and worship before you (Rev 15:4).

you alone are the Most High, Jesus Christ,

He will be great and will be called the son of the most high (Lk 1:32).

with the Holy Spirit, in the glory of God the Father. Amen.

—CCC 691–92

The Advocate, the holy Spirit that the Father will send in my name (Jn 14:26).

PROFESSION OF FAITH

All: We believe in one God, the Father, the Almighty, maker of heaven and earth,   —CCC 199–421
> . . . God most High, the creator of heaven and earth (Gen 14:19).

of all that is seen and unseen.   —CCC 325–54
> For in him were created all things in heaven and on earth, the visible and the invisible (Col 1:16).

We believe in one Lord, Jesus Christ, the only Son of God, eternally begotten of the Father,   —CCC 422–55
> Therefore the child to be born will be called holy, the Son of God (Lk 1:35).

God from God, Light from Light, true God from true God, begotten, not made, one in Being with the Father.
> . . .who is the refulgence of his glory, the very imprint of his being (Heb 1:3).

Through him all things were made.   —CCC 291
> In the beginning was the Word, / and the Word was with God, / and the Word was God. He was in the beginning with God. / All things came to be through him, / and without him nothing came to be. / What came to be through him was life, / and this life was the light of the human race (Jn 1:1–4).

For us men and for our salvation he came down from heaven: —CCC 456–60
> No one has gone up to heaven except the one who has come down from heaven, the Son of Man (Jn 3:13).

by the power of the Holy Spirit he was born of the Virgin Mary, and became man.   —CCC 461–63, 487ff.
> When his mother Mary was betrothed to Joseph, but before they lived together, she was found with child through the holy Spirit (Mt 1:18).

For our sake he was crucified under Pontius Pilate;
> Then he handed him over to them to be crucified (Jn 19:16).

he suffered, died, and was buried (CCC 571–630). On the third day he rose again in fulfillment of the Scriptures;
—CCC 638–58

For I handed on to you as of first importance what I also received: that Christ died for our sins in accordance with the Scriptures; that he was buried; that he was raised on the third day in accordance with the scriptures (1 Cor 15:3).

he ascended into heaven   —CCC 659–67

As he blessed them he parted from them and was taken up to heaven (Lk 24:51).

and is seated at the right hand of the Father.—CCC 663–64

. . . seek what is above, where Christ is seated at the right hand of God (Col 3:1).

He will come again in glory to judge the living and the dead,
—CCC 668–82

I charge you in the presence of God and of Christ Jesus, who will judge the living and the dead (2 Tim 4:1).

and his kingdom will have no end.

. . . and of his kingdom there will be no end (Lk 1:33).

We believe in the Holy Spirit, the Lord, the giver of life,
—CCC 683–747

"It shall come to pass in the last days," God says, / "that I will pour out a portion of my spirit upon all flesh" (Acts 2:17).

who proceeds from the Father and the Son. With the Father and the Son he is worshiped and glorified.

"and I will ask the Father, and he will give you another Advocate to be with you always . . ." (Jn 14:16).   —CCC 692

He has spoken through the Prophets.   —CCC 719

Concerning this salvation, prophets who prophesied about the grace that was to be yours searched and investigated it, investigating the time and circumstances that the Spirit of Christ within them indicated when it testified in advance to the sufferings destined for Christ and the glories to follow them (1 Pet 1:10–11).

We believe in one holy catholic and apostolic Church.
—CCC 811–70

... so we, though many, are one body in Christ and individually parts of one another (Rom 12:5).

We acknowledge one baptism for the forgiveness of sins.

—CCC 977–80

Repent and be baptized, every one of you, in the name of Jesus Christ for the forgiveness of your sins; . . . (Acts 2:38).

We look for the resurrection of the dead, and the life of the world to come. Amen.   —CCC 988–1060

For if we have grown into union with him through a death like his, we shall also be united with him in the resurrection (Rom 6:5).

Liturgy of the Eucharist

PREPARATION OF THE ALTAR AND GIFTS (CCC 1350)

Priest: Blessed are you, Lord, God of all creation. Through your goodness we have this bread to offer, which earth has given and human hands have made.   —CCC 1333

For every man, moreover, to eat and drink and enjoy the fruit of all his labor is a gift of God (Qo 3:13).

It will become for us the bread of life.

I am the bread of life; . . . (Jn 6:35).

Blessed are you, Lord, God of all creation. Through your goodness we have this wine to offer, fruit of the vine and work of human hands. It will become our spiritual drink.

—CCC 1333

Then he took a cup, gave thanks, and said: "Take this and share it among yourselves; for I tell you [that] from this time on I shall not drink of the fruit of the vine until the kingdom of God comes" (Lk 22:17–18).

People: Blessed be God for ever.

Blessed be God! (Ps 68:36).

Priest: Pray, brethren, that our sacrifice may be acceptable to God, the almighty Father.

Therefore, we who are receiving the unshakable kingdom should have gratitude, with which we should offer worship pleasing to God in reverence and awe (Heb 12:28).

People: May the Lord accept the sacrifice at your hands for the praise and glory of his name, for our good and the good of all his Church.   —CCC 1368

He that offers praise as a sacrifice glorifies me (Ps 50:23).

EUCHARISTIC PRAYER (CCC 1352–54)

Priest: Lift up your hearts.

People: We lift them up to the Lord.

Let us reach out our hearts toward God in heaven! (Lam 3:41).

Priest: Let us give thanks to the Lord our God.

. . . giving thanks to God the Father through him (Col 3:17).

People: It is right to give him thanks and praise.

We always give thanks to God, the Father of our Lord Jesus Christ (Col 1:3).

Preface changes with the feast.

PREFACE ACCLAMATION

All: Holy, holy, holy Lord, God of power and might, heaven and earth are full of your glory. Hosanna in the highest.

"Holy, holy, holy is the LORD of hosts!" they cried one to the other. "All the earth is filled with his glory!" (Is 6:3).

Blessed is he who comes in the name of the Lord. Hosanna in the highest.

Hosanna! / Blessed is he who comes in the name of the Lord! / . . . Hosanna in the highest! (Mk 12:9–10).

EUCHARISTIC PRAYER I

Priest: We come to you, Father, with praise and thanksgiving through Jesus Christ your Son.   —CCC 1359–61

. . . giving always and for everything in the name of our Lord Jesus Christ to God the Father (Eph 5:20).

Through him we ask you to accept and bless these gifts we offer you in sacrifice. —CCC 1334

> . . . accept this sacrifice on behalf of all your people Israel and guard and sanctify your heritage (2 Macc 1:26).

We offer them for your holy catholic Church, watch over it, Lord, and guide it; grant it peace and unity throughout the world. —CCC 820, 1398).

> . . . so that they may all be one, as you, Father, are in me and I in you (Jn 17:21).

We offer them for N., our Pope, and N., our bishop, and for all who hold and teach the catholic faith that comes to us from the apostles. —CCC 1369

> They devoted themselves to the teaching of the apostles and to the communal life, to the breaking of the bread and to the prayers (Acts 2:42).

Remember, Lord, your people, especially those for whom we now pray, N. and N. —CCC 960

Remember all of us gathered here before you. You know how firmly we believe in you and dedicate ourselves to you.

> Remember me, O LORD, as you favor your people; visit me with your saving help (Ps 106:4).

We offer you this sacrifice of praise for ourselves and those who are dear to us. —CCC 1361, 1368

> Through him [then] let us continually offer God a sacrifice of praise, that is, the fruit of lips that confess his name (Heb 13:15).

We pray to you, our living and true God, for our well-being and redemption.

In union with the whole Church —CCC 1369

At Christmas:

we celebrate that night when Mary without loss of her virginity gave the world its Savior. —CCC 496–507

> He had no relations with her until she bore a son, and he named him Jesus (Mt 1:25).

At Epiphany:

we celebrate that day when your only Son, sharing your eternal glory, showed himself in a human body.   —CCC 449

> . . . who, though he was in the form of God, / did not deem equality with God something to be grasped. / Rather, he emptied himself, / taking the form of a slave, / coming in human likeness (Phil 2:6–7).

General form:

we honor Mary, the ever-virgin mother [CCC 499–501] of Jesus Christ our Lord and God.

We honor Joseph, her husband,   —CCC 488

> . . . Jacob the father of Joseph, the husband of Mary (Mt 1:76).

the apostles and martyrs Peter and Paul, Andrew, James, John, Thomas, James, Philip, Bartholomew, Matthew, Simon and Jude; we honor Linus, Cletus, Clement, Sixtus, Cornelius, Cyprian, Lawrence, Chrysogonus, John and Paul, Cosmas and Damian and all the saints.

May their merits and prayers gain us your constant help and protection.   —CCC 956, 2683

Father, accept this offering from your whole family.

    —CCC 1369

Grant us your peace in this life, save us from final damnation, and count us among those you have chosen.

    —CCC 1392–93

> . . . strengthened with every power, in accord with his glorious might, for all endurance and patience, with joy giving thanks to the Father, who has made you fit to share the inheritance of the holy ones in light (Col 1:11).

Bless and approve our offering; make it acceptable to you, an offering in spirit and in truth.   —CCC 1179

> God is Spirit, and those who worship him must worship in Spirit and truth (Jn 4:24).

Let it become for us the body and blood of Jesus Christ your only Son, our Lord.   —CCC 1374ff.

The day before he suffered he took bread in his sacred hands and looking up to heaven, to you, his almighty Father, he gave you thanks and praise. He broke the bread, gave it to his disciples, and said: Take this, all of you, and eat it: this is my body which will be given up for you.

When supper was ended, he took the cup. Again he gave you thanks and praise, gave the cup to his disciples and said: Take this, all of you, and drink from it: this is the cup of my blood, the blood of the new and everlasting covenant. It will be shed for you and for all so that sins may be forgiven. Do this in memory of me.   —CCC 1353–54

> While they were eating, Jesus took bread, said the blessing, broke it, and giving it to his disciples said, "Take and eat; this is my body." Then he took a cup, gave thanks, and gave it to them, saying, "Drink from it, all of you, for this is my blood of the covenant, which will be shed on behalf of many for the forgiveness of sins" (Mt 26:26–28).

Let us proclaim the mystery of faith.

> Undeniably great is the mystery of devotion (1 Tim 3:16).

All: Christ has died, Christ is risen, Christ will come again.

> For I handed on to you as of first importance what I myself received: that Christ died for our sins in accordance with the scriptures; that he was buried; that he was raised on the third day in accordance with the scriptures (1 Cor 15:3–5).

Priest: Father, we celebrate the memory of Christ, your Son.
                              —CCC 1363–66

We, your people and your ministers, recall his passion, his resurrection from the dead, and his ascension into glory; and from the many gifts you have given us we offer to you, God of glory and majesty,

> . . . realizing that you were ransomed from your futile conduct, handed on by your ancestors, not with perishable things like silver or gold but with the precious blood of Christ as of a spotless unblemished lamb. He was known before the foundation of the world but revealed in the final time for you, who through him believe in God who raised him from the dead and gave him glory (1 Pet 1:18–21).

this holy and perfect sacrifice: —CCC 1367

> For if the blood of goats and bulls and the sprinkling of a heifer's ashes can sanctify those who are defiled so that their flesh is cleansed, how much more will the blood of Christ, who through the eternal spirit offered himself up unblemished to God, cleanse our consciences from dead works to worship the living God (Heb 9:13–14).

the bread of life and the cup of eternal salvation.

—CCC 1355, 1384

> Whoever eats my flesh and drinks my blood has eternal life, and I will raise him on the last day (Jn 6:54).

Look with favor on these offerings and accept them as once you accepted the gifts of your servant Abel,

> The LORD looked with favor on Abel and his offering (Gen 4:4).

the sacrifice of Abraham, our father in faith,

> "Do not lay your hand on the boy," said the messenger. "Do not do the least thing to him. I know now how devoted you are to God, since you did not withhold from me your own beloved son" (Gen 22:12).

and the bread and wine offered by your priest Melchisedech.

—CCC 1333

> Melchizedek, king of Salem, brought out bread and wine, and being a priest of God Most High, he blessed Abram (Gen 14:18).

Almighty God, we pray that your angel may take this sacrifice to your altar in heaven.

> Another angel came and stood at the altar, holding a gold censer. He was given a great quantity of incense to offer, along with the prayers of all the holy ones, on the gold altar that was before the throne. The smoke of the incense along with the prayers of the holy ones went up before God from the hand of the angel (Rev 8:3–4).

Then, as we receive from this altar the sacred body and blood of your Son, let us be filled with every grace and blessing.

—CCC 1402

> Blessed be the God and Father of our Lord Jesus Christ, who has blessed us in Christ with every spiritual blessing in the heavens (Eph 1:3).

Remember, Lord, those who have died and have gone before us marked with the sign of faith, especially those for whom we now pray, N. and N.   —CCC 1370

May these, and all who sleep in Christ, find in your presence light, happiness, and peace.   —CCC 1371

> We do not want you to be unaware, brothers, about those who have fallen asleep, so that you may not grieve like the rest, who have no hope. For if we believe that Jesus died and rose, so too will God, through Jesus, bring with him those who have fallen asleep (1 Th 4:13, 14).

For ourselves, too, we ask some share in the fellowship of your apostles and martyrs, with John the Baptist, Stephen, Matthias, Barnabas, Ignatius, Alexander, Marcellinus, Peter, Felicity, Perpetua, Agatha, Lucy, Agnes, Cecilia, Anastasia, and all the saints.   —CCC 1396

> . . . giving thanks to the Father, who has made you fit to share in the inheritance of the holy ones in light (Col 1:12).

Though we are sinners, we trust in your mercy and love. Do not consider what we truly deserve, but grant us your forgiveness.   —CCC 1380

> The sins of my youth and my frailties remember not; in your kindness remember me, because of your goodness, O Lord (Ps 25:7).

Through Christ our Lord. Through him you give us all these gifts. You fill them with life and goodness, you bless them and make them holy.

> They all look to you to give them food in due time. When you give it to them, they gather it; when you open your hand, they are filled with good things (Ps 104:27–28).

EUCHARISTIC PRAYER II

Priest: Lord, you are holy indeed, the fountain of all holiness.

> Therefore, O holy One, Lord of all holiness, preserve forever undefiled this house, which has been so recently purified (2 Macc 14:36).

Let your Spirit come upon these gifts to make them holy, so that they may become for us the body and blood of our Lord, Jesus Christ.   —CCC 1353

Before he was given up to death,

> . . . he humbled himself, becoming obedient to death, even death on a cross (Phil 2:8).

a death he freely accepted,

> This is why the Father loves me, because I lay down my life in order to take it up again. No one takes it from me, but I lay it down on my own. I have power to lay it down, and power to take it up again (Jn 10:17–18).

he took bread and gave you thanks. He broke the bread, gave it to his disciples, and said: Take this, all of you, and eat it: this is my body which will be given up for you.

—CCC 1339, 1374

When supper was ended, he took the cup. Again he gave you thanks and praise, gave the cup to his disciples, and said: Take this, all of you, and drink from it: this is the cup of my blood, the blood of the new and everlasting covenant. It will be shed for you and for all so that sins may be forgiven. Do this in memory of me.

> While they were eating, he took bread, said the blessing, broke it, and gave it to them, and said, "Take it; this is my body." Then he took a cup, gave thanks, and gave it to them, and they all drank from it. He said to them, "This is my blood of the covenant, which will be shed for many" (Mk 14:22–25).

Let us proclaim the mystery of faith.

All: Dying you destroyed our death, rising you restored our life, Lord Jesus, come in glory.

> Now since the children share in blood and flesh, he likewise shared in them, that through death he might destroy the one who has the power of death, that is, the devil, and free those who through fear of death had been subject to slavery all their life (Heb 2:14–15).

Priest: In memory of his death and resurrection, we offer you, Father, this life-giving bread, this saving cup.   —CCC 1355

I am the living bread that came down from heaven; whoever eats this bread will live forever; and the bread that I will give is my flesh for the life of the world (Jn 6:51).

We thank you for counting us worthy to stand in your presence and serve you. —CCC 1386

May all of us who share in the body and blood of Christ be brought together in unity by the Holy Spirit. —CCC 1396

Because the loaf of bread is one, we, though many, are one body, for we all partake of the one loaf (1 Cor 10:17).

Lord, remember your Church throughout the world; make us grow in love, together with N., our Pope, N., our bishop, and all the clergy. —CCC 1369

Remember our brothers and sisters who have gone to their rest in the hope of rising again: bring them and all the departed into the light of your presence. —CCC 1371

. . . it was a holy and pious thought. Thus he made atonement for the dead that they might be freed from this sin (2 Macc 12:45–46).

Have mercy on us all; make us worthy to share eternal life with Mary, the virgin Mother of God, with the apostles, and with all the saints who have done your will throughout the ages. —CCC 1402ff.

May we praise you in union with them, and give you glory through your Son, Jesus Christ.

. . . the afflictions you endure. This is evidence of the just judgment of God, so that you may be considered worthy of the kingdom of God (2 Th 1:4–5).

EUCHARISTIC PRAYER III

Priest: Father, you are holy indeed, and all creation rightly gives you praise.

Let the heavens and all your creation praise you forever (Tob 8:5).

All life, all holiness comes from you through your Son, Jesus Christ our Lord, by the working of the Holy Spirit.

—CCC 291

> All things came to be through him, and without him nothing came to be (Jn 1:3).

From age to age you gather a people to yourself, so that from east to west a perfect offering may be made to the glory of your name.

> From the rising to the setting of the sun is the name of the LORD to be praised (Ps 113:3).

And so, Father, we bring you these gifts. We ask you to make them holy by the power of your Spirit, that they may become the body and blood of your Son, our Lord Jesus Christ, at whose command we celebrate this eucharist.   —CCC 1353 On the night he was betrayed, he took bread and gave you thanks and praise. He broke the bread, gave it to his disciples, and said: Take this, all of you, and eat it: this is my body which will be given up for you.

When supper was ended, he took the cup. Again he gave you thanks and praise, gave the cup to his disciples, and said: Take this, all of you, and drink from it: this is the cup of my blood, the blood of the new and everlasting covenant. It will be shed for you and for all so that sins may be forgiven. Do this in memory of me.   —CCC 1353, 1374ff.

> Then he took the bread, said the blessing, broke it, and gave it to them, saying, "This is my body, which will be given for you; do this in memory of me." And likewise the cup after they had eaten, saying, "This cup is the new covenant in my blood, which will be shed for you" (Lk 22:19–20).

Let us proclaim the mystery of faith.

All: When we eat this bread and drink this cup, we proclaim your death, Lord Jesus, until you come in glory.

—CCC 1076, 1344, 1393, 2776

> For as often as you eat this bread and drink this cup, you proclaim the death of the Lord until he comes (1 Cor 11:26).

Priest: Father, calling to mind the death your Son endured for our salvation, his glorious resurrection and ascension into heaven, and ready to greet him when he comes again, we offer you in thanksgiving this holy and living sacrifice.

—CCC 1362ff.

Be watchful! Be alert! You do not know when the time will come (Mk 13:33).

Look with favor on your Church's offering, and see the Victim whose death has reconciled us to yourself.

—CCC 1367ff.

. . . namely, God was reconciling the world to himself in Christ, not counting their trespasses against them and entrusting to us the message of reconciliation (2 Cor 5:19).

Grant that we, who are nourished by his body and blood, may be filled with his Holy Spirit, and become one body, one spirit in Christ.   —CCC 1396

. . . striving to preserve the unity of the Spirit through the bond of peace (Eph 4:3).

May he make us an everlasting gift to you and enable us to share in the inheritance of your saints, with Mary, the virgin Mother of God; with the apostles, the martyrs, and all your saints, on whose constant intercession we rely for help.

—CCC 1402ff.

Husbands, love your wives, even as Christ loved the church and handed himself over for her to sanctify her, cleansing her by the bath of water with the word, that he might present to himself the church in splendor (Eph 5:25–27).

Lord, may this sacrifice, which has made our peace with you, advance the peace and salvation of all the world.

—CCC 1366–67

Strengthen in faith and love your pilgrim Church on earth; your servant Pope N., our bishop N., and all the bishops, with the clergy and the entire people your Son has gained for you.

—CCC 1369

Father, hear the prayers of the family you have gathered here before you. In mercy and love unite all your children wherever they may be.

> I have given them the glory you gave me, so that they may be one, as we are one, I in them and you in me, that they may be brought to perfection as one (Jn 17:22, 23).

Welcome into your kingdom our departed brothers and sisters, and all who have left this world in your friendship.

—CCC 1371

We hope to enjoy for ever the vision of your glory, through Christ our Lord, from whom all good things come.

—CCC 1402ff.

> . . . for we have heard of your faith in Christ Jesus and the love that you have for all the holy ones, because of the hope reserved for you in heaven (Col 1:4–5).

EUCHARISTIC PRAYER IV

Priest: Father, we acknowledge your greatness: all your actions show your wisdom and love.

You formed man in your own likeness and set him over the whole world to serve you, his creator, and to rule over all creatures.   —CCC 355–84

> Then God said: "Let us make man in our image, after our likeness. Let them have dominion over the fish of the sea, the birds of the air, and the cattle, and over all the wild animals and all the creatures that crawl on the ground" (Gen 1:26).

Even when he disobeyed you and lost your friendship you did not abandon him to the power of death, but helped all men to seek and to find you.   —CCC 410–21

> Seek the Lord while he may be found, call him while he is near (Is 55:6).

Again and again you offered a covenant to man, and through the prophets taught him to hope for salvation.

> Come to me heedfully, listen, that you may have life. I will renew

with you the everlasting covenant, the benefits assured to David (Is 55:3).

Father, you so loved the world that in the fullness of time you sent your only Son to be our Savior. —CCC 422–51

But when the fullness of time had come, God sent his Son, born of a woman, born under the law, to ransom those under the law, so that we might receive adoption (Gal 4:4–5).

He was conceived through the power of the Holy Spirit, and born of the Virgin Mary, a man like us in all things but sin. —CCC 456–511

For we do not have a high priest who is unable to sympathize with our weakness, but one who has similarly been tested in every way, yet without sin (Heb 4:15).

To the poor he proclaimed the good news of salvation, to prisoners, freedom, and to those in sorrow, joy. —CCC 543–46

The spirit of the Lord is upon me, / because he has anointed me / to bring glad tidings to the poor. / He has sent me to proclaim liberty to captives / and recovery of sight to the blind, / to let the oppressed go free (Lk 4:18).

In fulfillment of your will he gave himself up to death; but by rising from the dead, he destroyed death and restored life. —CCC 571–658

"Death is swallowed up in victory. / Where, O death, is your victory? / Where, O death, is your sting?". . . But thanks be to God who gives us the victory through our Lord Jesus Christ (1 Cor 15:54–57).

And that we might live no longer for ourselves but for him, he sent the Holy Spirit from you, Father, as his first gift to those who believe, to complete his work on earth and bring us the fullness of grace. —CCC 683–810

And I will ask the Father and he will give you another Advocate—to be with you always . . . (Jn 14:16).

Father, may this Holy Spirit sanctify these offerings. —CCC 1353

Let them become the body and blood of Jesus Christ our Lord as we celebrate the great mystery which he left us as an everlasting covenant.

> For this reason he is mediator of a new covenant: since a death has taken place for deliverance from transgressions under the first covenant, those who are called may receive the promised eternal inheritance (Heb 9:15).

He always loved those who were his own in the world. When the time came for him to be glorified by you, his heavenly Father, he showed the depth of his love.

> He loved his own in the world and he loved them to the end (Jn 13:1).

While they were at supper, he took bread, said the blessing, broke the bread, and gave it to his disciples, saying: Take this, all of you, and eat it: this is my body which will be given up for you.

In the same way, he took the cup, filled with wine. He gave you thanks, and giving the cup to his disciples, said: Take this, all of you, and drink from it: this is the cup of my blood, the blood of the new and everlasting covenant. It will be shed for you and for all so that sins may be forgiven. Do this in memory of me.   —CCC 1353, 1374ff.

> For I received from the Lord what I also handed on to you, that the Lord Jesus, on the night he was handed over, took bread and, after he had given thanks, broke it and said, "This is my body that is for you. Do this in remembrance of me." In the same way also the cup, after supper, saying, "This cup is the new covenant in my blood. Do this, as often as you drink it, in remembrance of me" (1 Cor 11:23–25).

Let us proclaim the mystery of faith.

All: Lord, by your cross and resurrection, you have set us free. You are the Savior of the world.

> . . . for we have heard for ourselves, and we know that this is truly the savior of the world (Jn 4:42).

Priest: Father, we now celebrate this memorial of our re-

demption. We recall Christ's death, his descent among the
dead,   —CCC 632–37, 1362ff.

> Put to death in the flesh, he was brought to life in the spirit. In it he
> also went to preach to the spirits in prison (1 Pet 3:18, 19).

his resurrection, and his ascension to your right hand [CCC
638–67];

> . . . in accord with the exercise of his great might, which he worked
> in Christ, raising him from the dead and seating him at his right hand
> in the heavens (Eph 1:19–20).

and, looking forward to his coming in glory,   —CCC 668–82

> When the Son of Man comes in his glory, and all the angels with
> him, he will sit upon his glorious throne (Mt 25:31).

we offer you his body and blood, the acceptable sacrifice
which brings salvation to the whole world.   —CCC 1367
Lord, look upon this sacrifice which you have given to your
Church; and by your Holy Spirit, gather all who share this
one bread and one cup into the one body of Christ, a living
sacrifice of praise.   —CCC 1368, 1396

> As a body is one though it has many parts, and all the parts of the
> body, though many, are one body, so also Christ. . . . Now you are
> Christ's body, and individually parts of it (1 Cor 12:12, 27).

Lord, remember those for whom we offer this sacrifice, especially N., our Pope, N., our bishop, and bishops and clergy
everywhere.   —CCC 1369
Remember those who take part in this offering, those here
present and all your people, and all who seek you with a sincere heart.

> Rather, the man of any nation who fears God and acts uprightly is
> acceptable to him (Acts 10:35).

Remember those who have died in the peace of Christ and
all the dead whose faith is known to you alone.

                                             —CCC 1371

Father, in your mercy grant also to us, your children, to enter
into our heavenly inheritance in the company of the Virgin

Mary, the Mother of God, and your apostles and saints.

—CCC 1402ff.

Then, in your kingdom, freed from the corruption of sin and death, we shall sing your glory with every creature through Christ our Lord, through whom you give us everything that is good.

> . . . in hope that creation itself will be set free from slavery to corruption and share in the glorious freedom of the children of God (Rom 8:20–21).

DOXOLOGY

Priest: Through him, with him, in him, in the unity of the Holy Spirit, all glory and honor is yours, almighty Father, for ever and ever.

People: Amen.   —CCC 1103

> For from him and through him and for him are all things. To him be glory forever. Amen (Rom 11:36).

Communion Rite

LORD'S PRAYER (CCC 2777–854)

All: Our Father, who art in heaven, hallowed be thy name; thy kingdom come; thy will be done on earth as it is in heaven. Give us this day our daily bread; and forgive us our trespasses as we forgive those who trespass against us; and lead us not into temptation, but deliver us from evil.

> Our Father in heaven, / hallowed be your name, / your kingdom come, / your will be done, / on earth as it is in heaven. / Give us today our daily bread; / and forgive us our debts, / as we forgive our debtors; / and do not subject us to the final test, / but deliver us from the evil one (Mt 6:9–13).

Priest: Deliver us, Lord, from every evil, and grant us peace in our day. In your mercy keep us free from sin and protect us from all anxiety as we wait in joyful hope for the coming of our Savior, Jesus Christ.

> I do not ask that you take them out of the world but that you keep them from the evil one (Jn 17:15).

People: For the kingdom, the power, and the glory are yours, now and for ever.   —CCC 2855

> *Didaché* (Teaching of the Apostles, first century).

Priest: Lord Jesus Christ, you said to your apostles: I leave you peace, my peace I give you. Look not on our sins, but on the faith of your Church, and grant us the peace and unity of your kingdom where you live for ever and ever.

> Peace I leave with you; my peace I give to you . . . (Jn 14:27).

Priest: The peace of the Lord be with you always.

> Peace be with you (Jn 20:19).

BREAKING OF THE BREAD

People: Lamb of God, you take away the sins of the world: have mercy on us.

Lamb of God, you take away the sins of the world: have mercy on us.

Lamb of God, you take away the sins of the world: grant us peace.

> The next day he saw Jesus coming toward him and said "Behold, the Lamb of God who takes away the sin of the world" (Jn 1:29).

COMMUNION

Priest: This is the Lamb of God who takes away the sins of the world. Happy are those who are called to his supper.

> Blessed are those who have been called to the wedding feast of the Lamb (Rev 19:9).

All: Lord, I am not worthy to receive you, but only say the word and I shall be healed.   —CCC 1386

> Lord, I am not worthy to have you enter under my roof; only say the word and my servant will be healed (Mt 8:8).

DISMISSAL

[Pontifical Blessing]

Priest: Blessed be the name of the Lord.

People: Now and forever.

Blessed be the name of God forever and ever (Dan 2:20).

Priest: Our help is in the name of the Lord.

People: Who made heaven and earth.

Our help is in the name of the LORD, who made heaven and earth (Ps 124:8).

Priest: May almighty God bless you, the Father, and the Son, and the Holy Spirit.

As he blessed them he parted from them and was taken up to heaven (Lk 24:51).

Priest: (a) Go in the peace of Christ.

Your faith has saved you; go in peace (Lk 7:50).

(b) The Mass is ended, go in peace.   —CCC 1332

(c) Go in peace to love and serve the Lord.

Serve now the LORD, your God, and his people Israel (2 Chron 35:3).

People: Thanks be to God.

Thanks be to God for his indescribable gift! (2 Cor 9:15).

V

"What About . . . ?"

In a book like this, which is centered on certain large themes, some smaller but equally problematic topics can get over-looked. In this last chapter, therefore, I have assembled the most frequently raised questions on a wide range of biblically related topics. In many instances, the answers merely scratch the surface but should serve as a means to direct the reader to additional personal reflection, research, and study.

1. *Why do Catholics place the Church above the Bible?*
Catholics do not place the Church above the Bible. As a matter of fact, the Second Vatican Council declared that the Church "venerates" the Scriptures (CCC 103; see also 86). How does one venerate something beneath oneself?

The Church extends many visible signs of this reverence for the Word of God, especially in the liturgy. The lectionary is carried in solemn procession; the Book of the Gospels is flanked by candles, is incensed, and even kissed. Why is all this done? Because the Church sees in the Scriptures a very special gift of God's revelation to His people. As such it provides the Church with a clear and definitive norm for her to judge her actions and fidelity.

That having been said, we may add that Catholics do not

view the Scriptures as self–explanatory but as requiring the community that formed the Bible to interpret it. After all, we know that were it not for the Church, there would be no Bible, for it was the Church that sifted through the books claiming divine inspiration and came up with the books that now serve as the canon, or definitive list of works regarded as divinely inspired and worthy of incorporation into what is now the Bible (CCC 120).

It is important to recall, however, that this process did not occur overnight. The ancient Hebrews went through this process for their Scriptures, and the Church took nearly four centuries to come up with a standard catalogue. This kind of historical background is needed to provide believers with a sense of balance, which avoids the extreme of disregarding the Scriptures as well as the extreme of making extravagant claims for the Scriptures, which even the apostolic Church would have rejected.

2. Didn't the Catholic Church for centuries—particularly before the Protestant Reformation—try to keep the Bible from the people?
To answer this question calls for a little historical investigation.

First of all, Christians did not possess the Bible as we now know it until the fourth century. A variety of writings claiming apostolic authority were in circulation, and only gradually did the Church come to decide on the precise books that could be accepted as inspired and canonical (CCC 120), in much the same way as Judaism established the Old Testament canon in the last quarter of the first century of the Christian era.

Second, for the next twelve centuries, even if the Church had given a copy of the Bible to every Catholic, little good would have been accomplished, because the vast majority of the world's people were illiterate.

Third, having personal copies of the Bible became a possibility only with Johann Gutenberg's invention of printing from movable types in 1456. Interestingly enough, the first book printed by Gutenberg (a Catholic) was the Bible—more than sixty years before Luther's revolt!

Fourth, private ownership of a Bible was still but a remote possibility because of the tremendous cost of printing. Some scholars estimate that in 1456 a printed Bible would have cost as much as eight thousand dollars in current exchange.

However, until the advent of the printing press and of more general literacy, monks preserved the Bible through painstaking hand-copying of the texts. These beautifully illuminated manuscripts (many of which are on display in museums around the world) were then placed in libraries and chained to lecterns—not to keep people from them, but to guarantee their availability.

3. *Why weren't Catholics allowed to read the Bible even in the years just prior to Vatican Council II?*
They *were*, and I can speak from personal experience, since I was a schoolboy in those days. Much earlier, as soon as Bibles became more accessible and as literacy rates rose, the Church not only permitted but encouraged her sons and daughters to read the Scriptures.

When I was a parochial-school student in the 1950s, at least one hour each week was spent on biblical studies. This was in addition to our regular catechism classes, which incorporated scriptural citations to ground Catholic teachings in the Bible. Still more time was spent on studying the Gospel passages used at Sunday Mass. I can distinctly remember receiving the gift of a New Testament for my confirmation at the age of eleven.

All of this autobiographical information is offered to make a point, namely, that the Church's strong endorsement of Scripture reading and study for Catholics did not come out of the blue but was the logical conclusion of a gradual but determined course of action, for which the Church had been preparing believers for decades and even centuries (CCC 131–33).

4. *Why are Catholics ignorant of Scripture?*
Naturally, to be fair, one would have to modify the question to speak of "some Catholics", for a group indictment would be very wrong and inaccurate.

Many Catholics are ignorant of the Scriptures for the same reason that they are ignorant of a whole variety of faith-related matters: a lack of education. Some of this ignorance is no fault of their own but the result of a lack in family environment or not having access to a Catholic education. Other Catholics may have doctorate degrees but a second-grade understanding of their faith, and so we find a conscious decision to remain ignorant.

Some Catholics know a great deal about the Bible, but they do not have this knowledge arranged in any kind of systematic format. They have obtained this information by osmosis rather than through organized classes. Although they may not be able to cite chapter and verse, as can some non-Catholics (and I stress *some*), they are surely conversant with the characters and themes of both Testaments.

Interestingly enough, recent surveys demonstrate that Catholics and Protestants have no appreciable differences among them in being able to name the four evangelists or twelve apostles; all are rather poor! However, the Church since Vatican II has committed herself to "opening wide" the Scriptures to the faithful, on the premise that Saint Jerome many centuries earlier was correct in asserting that "ignorance of the Scriptures is ignorance of Christ" (CCC 133; 1792).

5. *Why don't Catholics hear about Scripture in the Mass and in their schools?*
Myths die hard. It seems that once an image or idea is impressed on the minds of some people (regardless of how inaccurate it is), they refuse to be disabused of it. In a sense, they are saying, "Please don't confuse me with the facts."

As earlier chapters make clear, the Mass is the most biblical prayer imaginable. The entire first half of the Mass is almost nothing but pure, unadulterated Bible-reading and commentary. The second half contains direct quotations from Scripture (see Chapter IV) as well as biblical allusions (CCC 1346, 1349). The heart of the Liturgy of the Eucharist is nothing other than a ritual action performed in obedience to the Lord's command on the night before He died—a command clearly documented in the Scriptures.

Catholic education is permeated with the Scriptures, both directly in course work and indirectly in an overall meshing of the Word with the study of liturgy, doctrine, and morality. I would challenge anyone to prove otherwise, so sure and proud am I of this claim.

6. *Why do Catholics seem more interested in the teachings of philosophers such as Saint Thomas Aquinas than in the direct message of the Bible itself?*
Catholics are not more interested in Aquinas than in the Bible. They are interested in the pursuit of truth, which comes about when people investigate reality from a variety of angles.

Rational beings have always held that all truth is one; therefore, it is not correct to separate sacred truth from secular truth. In fact, the acquisition of what may appear to be merely secular knowledge can be extremely beneficial in increasing one's appreciation of the Word of God. That is why Catholic biblical scholars are trained in many fields: linguistics, anthropology, archaeology, history.

The study of philosophy reveals what man, unaided by grace and revelation, can comprehend of the mystery of life and even of God. The Church then adds the dimension of faith to that and evolves the science of theology, enabling us to grow in our understanding of both divine and human realities (CCC 31–38).

The biblical authors themselves had a wide range of human knowledge; this is especially evident when one turns to the wisdom literature or the writings of Saint Paul, which have been rather heavily influenced by Greek (pagan) philosophy.

7. What are the differences between the Catholic and Protestant Bibles, and why?

This is a very complex matter, calling for very careful analysis. As a brief response, we can say that the Protestant Bible lacks seven books that are a part of the Catholic version of the Old Testament (CCC 120). These books are: Tobit, Judith, Wisdom, Sirach, Baruch, 1 Maccabees, and 2 Maccabees. But why?

For many years prior to the coming of Christ, the Jews used two different versions of their own Scriptures, depending on the part of the world in which they lived. The Scriptures used by the Greek-speaking Jews outside Palestine contained the seven books in question, while the Bible in use in Palestine did not. When Saint Jerome undertook to translate the Bible into Latin, he used the Greek Septuagint version and thus had the fuller canon before him. When Protestants in the sixteenth century began to make their own translations of the Scriptures, they began with the Palestinian canon, which lacked those seven works.

We do know, however, that apparently the apostolic Church relied on the Septuagint text because quotations from the Hebrew Scriptures used in the New Testament come from that source. We also know that Luther favored the Palestinian canon over the Septuagint because 2 Maccabees implies belief in the existence of purgatory, a doctrine he detested. Thus, by opting for the other canon, he was not confronted with a scriptural warranty for purgatory. But Luther was not above deleting inconvenient books from the New Testament either, as he did with Hebrews, James, Jude, and Revelation.

Increasingly, one finds Protestant scholarship growing more accepting of the Catholic canon of the Bible because it is based on good, reliable, historical evidence. As a result, many Protestant Bibles now include the so-called "apocryphal books", even if at the end.

8. *What do Catholics have against the King James Bible?*

Catholics have nothing "against" the King James Bible, per se. No one could fault this version of the Scriptures on its beauty of language and majesty of expression. Catholic objections are based on several other concerns, however.

First of all is the fact that it is an incomplete version of the Hebrew Scriptures, as already discussed in answer to the preceding question.

Second is the absence of critical notes to help readers understand troublesome passages or even what might seem to be conflicting passages.

A third objection may surprise many, and it is that the King James Bible is a rather poor translation, in spite of its high and lofty tone. In the nineteenth century, Protestant Scripture scholars convened in St. Louis to work toward a better translation, because the King James version had been found to have more than thirty thousand errors in it!

No translation is perfect, because fallible humans and limited human languages are involved. Nevertheless, the goal should be constantly to seek to improve upon previous editions, especially as our knowledge of ancient languages and texts increases.

Catholics in the United States are most familiar with the Jerusalem Bible, the New American Bible, and, increasingly, the Revised Standard Version. Since Vatican II, ecumenical teams of scholars have collaborated on many translations of great value, including the Common Bible. Such ecumenical cooperation is very desirable, since it moves us toward the use of one Bible as a common point of departure for conversations that have Christian unity for their aim.

9. *How can a teaching like the Assumption of Mary be required for belief when it is nowhere mentioned in Scripture?*

Simply because a teaching is not explicitly taught in the Bible does not mean it is untrue or that it is not there implicitly, waiting to be uncovered by the Church's reflection on God's Word. It is necessary to recall also that the Church does not feel bound to the dictum of *sola Scriptura* (Scripture alone), because we believe that God has revealed Himself to us through both Scripture and Tradition (CCC 78, 80–83). Some examples might be helpful.

Nowhere in the New Testament can one find the word "Trinity", yet no one espousing a Bible-based form of Christianity would hesitate to speak of the Godhead as a Trinity of Persons. Why? Because the doctrine of the Trinity is implicitly taught in a variety of passages, even if not explicitly so.

What has often happened is that some non-Catholic Christians have had problems with various tenets of the Catholic faith and then concluded a nonexistence of scriptural support. At the same time, the Church has always believed that the silence of Scripture on certain matters opens the door to freedom. This is certainly the case in regard to the Marian doctrines of the Immaculate Conception (CCC 491–92) and Assumption (CCC 966). Taught in seminal form in the New Testament (see Lk 1 and Rev 12), constantly believed by the Church from earliest times, and nowhere denied in Scripture, the Church's meditation on these mysteries led to clearly defined dogmas (see CCC 487).

It should be noted also that dogmatic definition is not an everyday occurrence in the Church, contrary to the opinion held by many outside the Church.

10. *For whom was the Bible written?*
The Bible was written by people of faith as a testimony to God's mighty deeds accomplished in Israel and in the person of His Son. Hence, it was intended to arouse others to faith. The Scriptures are also meant to sustain faith in one who already believes. Faith, then, is the thread running throughout.

However, even an agnostic (CCC 2127–28) or atheist can benefit from reading the Scriptures as long as he does not consciously block out divine grace or go to the Bible for the wrong reason (for example, to seek scientific data). The Bible can both console and challenge, and it must be allowed to do both, for "God's word is living and effective, sharper than any two-edged sword" (Heb 4:12).

11. *Does the Bible contradict itself?*

Contradiction is a facet of falsehood. God, Who is Truth, can never partake in falsehood, and hence His Word as revealed in the Scriptures can never present contradictory "truths" (CCC 107).

At times, we are face to face with an apparent or seeming contradiction in Scripture, but deeper investigation usually uncovers the deeper truth that first eluded us.

At other times, a defective method of biblical interpretation is at fault. For example, if one engages in "proof-texting", one is bound to turn up numerous verses that look as though they contradict one another. However, the use of isolated texts to prove a point is methodologically flawed; one must always place a particular passage in context, so that the true meaning can be perceived.

As Catholics, we believe the Scriptures are God's inspired Word and therefore inerrant (CCC 105–8). History, theology, philosophy, linguistics, and archaeology are all important aids in biblical interpretation. Most important of all, however, is a willingness to benefit from the Church's experience in this area, as she has assisted the faithful for two thousand years in coming to an appreciation of the truth of the Bible. The Holy Spirit, Who guided the sacred authors in committing the divine message to written form, similarly guides the Church in her interpretation of that revealed Word, which is not always easy to understand but is always true, as God is true.

12. *What did Jesus mean when He said everyone must be
"born again"? Can "born-again" people sin and lose out
on heaven?*

John 3:3 is the verse in question. Jesus was indicating that, because of our fallen nature, it is necessary to be "born again" of water and the Holy Spirit—a reference to baptism, which incorporates a believer into Christ and His Church (see Rom 5 and 6; 1 Cor 12; CCC 782, 1265ff.).

While baptism removes original sin, it does not remove the human inclination to sin. Hence the logical question: "How do I know I am saved?" No absolute assurance is available; one must have recourse to the virtue of hope, which is a firm trust in God's goodness and mercy. Some Fundamentalists hold that someone who is saved "knows" for sure, but Saint Paul had different ideas on the subject. He said the Philippians needed to "work out [their] salvation with fear and trembling" (2:12). Paul likewise warned against presumption in this matter: "Therefore, whoever thinks he is standing secure should take care not to fall" (1 Cor 10:12). Certainly this was also the mind of Christ, Who counseled constant vigilance as the best preparation for His coming (for example, Mt 25).

13. *What does it mean to "have a personal relationship with Jesus Christ"?*
The expression can mean a great deal, very little, or nothing at all. Some people speak of having a personal relationship with the Lord in such a way as to suggest that Jesus could be one's "buddy"; blasphemy or presumption are involved when one reduces the sovereign Lord to the level of the manipulable.

On the other hand, Saint Paul indicates that through baptism a believer is incorporated into Christ, with a real union resulting (CCC 1267–70). The initial relationship is then nourished through prayer, the Scriptures, and the sacraments, especially the Eucharist.

A relationship with Christ, then, is essential for every Christian. The only caution is that the transcendence of God (His absolute otherness) be kept in view as one enjoys the benefits of His immanence (His nearness revealed in Christ).

Questions to test for balance are: Do I feel as though I am known and loved by Christ as an individual? Do I hear His challenge to grow into His image more and more, leaving sin behind?

14. *What kind of an answer is appropriate to give to an Assemblies of God member who says "organized religion" is unnecessary and contrary to the Bible?*

Anti-institutional postures are not new in Christianity. Centuries ago, Saint Cyprian reacted to the very same attitude when he wisely noted that "no one can have God for his Father who will not have the Church for his mother" (CCC 181).

The Incarnation was a scandal to Jews and Greeks alike; the very thought that God could become man was just a bit much. When Jesus spoke of giving His flesh in the Eucharist, still others found it all too much, so they "no longer accompanied him" (Jn 6:66).

The Incarnation is continued in the Church (CCC 787ff.), so it should come as no surprise that people should find this manifestation of God in the flesh just as much a stumbling block. Some people are scandalized by the all-too-human face of the Church; others fear that an embodied presence of Christ in the world might make too many demands on them.

Regardless of the motivation, it is clear that Christianity without the Church is theologically impossible (see 1 Cor 12). It is also sociologically impossible, and the best proof of that is that even an anti-institutional Christian like a member of the Assemblies of God is a member of an institution for the simple reason that people need community, a fact acknowledged and accepted by our Lord in declaring His intention to build His Church on the rock of Peter (see Mt 16:18).

15. *What does the Church teach about the Book of Revelation? Does that book teach that the Pope is the anti-Christ and that Catholics bear the mark of the beast?*
The Book of Revelation is the last book of the Bible, perhaps the most discussed, and at the same time the least understood (CCC 120).

It belongs to that genre of literature known as apocalyptic because of its concern with visions and dreams. Like the Book of Daniel in the Hebrew Scriptures, it abounds in figurative and symbolic language, which was particularly important to keep its contents from being understood if the work fell into the wrong hands (that is, the authorities of the Roman Empire, who were persecuting the Church so fiercely at the time of its writing). In other words, it was written in "code", with numbers and animals all assigned a specific meaning.

A favorite section of this biblical book for many anti-Catholics is chapter 17, with its many references to Rome as the whore of Babylon and to the anti-Christ and the beast (CCC 675–76). Even a superficial reading of these passages would reveal that the Pope and the Church of Rome are hardly intended here, but instead the Roman emperor (perhaps Domitian, who reigned from A.D. 81 to 96) and indeed the entire Roman system, which was attempting to destroy the Church at Rome, as it had already killed Rome's first bishop, Saint Peter. If these Catholic-baiters were not so serious about their alleged scriptural proof for the condemnation of Catholicism, the irony would be amusing. Standard rules of interpretation and an objective view of history, however, will not substantiate their claims.

16. *Should Catholics attend non-Catholic Bible study programs?*

No one answer can be given; it will depend on who the teacher is and who the student is. Let me explain.

Studying the Bible with other Christians can be an enriching experience if the course is based on solid scholarship, which takes account of the culture, historical setting, and literary forms of the particular age that produced the work under study (see CCC 95). Thus excessive literalism is out of the question. One should also be wary of Scripture study that tries to use the Bible to "prove" the validity of a sectarian viewpoint; Fundamentalists whose principal objective is proselytizing come to mind immediately.

A student who has a poor grounding in his Catholic faith would be ill-advised to join an ecumenical study group for two reasons. First, such a person could make no significant contribution to ecumenical dialogue. Second, such a person will only become confused and risk loss of faith. The solution in this case, of course, is for the person to make up the gaps in his Catholic education.

17. *How do I handle Seventh-Day Adventists, Assemblies of God people, or Jehovah's Witnesses who come to my door proselytizing?*

People who are so committed to their beliefs that they seek to make converts are to be admired. Problems surface, however, when they are either misinformed or bigoted.

It seems to me that Catholics should welcome anyone as Christ, but that same principle also suggests that the guest is acting in Christlike charity. My own father always relished opportunities to engage in dialogue with door-to-door missionaries, because he saw such moments as opportunities to share his faith with them. I know of at least one visitor whom he led into the fullness of Christian faith found in the Catholic Church (CCC 855–56).

Dialogue is one thing; harassment is another. When individuals become offensive, they have ceased to act in a Christlike manner; they have thus worn out their welcome and should be shown to the door, courteously but firmly.

It is a good idea always to have on hand some Catholic pamphlets on a variety of topics to offer non-Catholic missionaries, especially pamphlets designed to answer the most common questions or objections regarding Catholicism.

A Catholic who does not know his faith well should do two things: keep the door closed; remedy the deficiencies.

18. *Why do Catholics pray to the saints, when the Bible tells us Jesus is the sole mediator between God and man?*
Catholics agree that Jesus is the sole mediator between God and man (CCC 618, 1544), but that belief in no way makes prayer to the saints useless or wrong.

Many times one finds the New Testament recommending intercessory prayer (see Col 1:9; 2 Th 1:11; 2 Th 3:1; James 5:16), and very few Christians seem to have a problem with seeking the prayers of a fellow believer. A difficulty appears to emerge only when that believer has left this earth. But what difference should that make to one who affirms the resurrection of the dead? After all, we read that all are alive in Christ (see 1 Cor 15:22; CCC 954–62).

To recap, then: The teaching of the Church is clear: Jesus Christ is the sole mediator between God and man. No other person in heaven or on earth can take His place. The role of Mary or any other saint is to lead the believer to Christ. This subordinate form of mediation derives its meaning and efficacy from the Lord Himself and is not something the saints possess on their own.

Intercessory prayer is a powerful expression of the beautiful doctrine of the communion of saints, whereby the saints in heaven, the souls in purgatory, and the faithful on earth are involved and concerned with one another's eternal salvation. Intercessory prayer declares our love for one another in the Church as well as our faith that the bonds to Christ and His Church forged in baptism cannot be dissolved by death (CCC 1267ff.).

Conclusion

When Catholics are accused of not knowing their Bible, they should have one of two reactions. The first should be to take offense if it is not true. The second should be to remedy the situation if it is true. Catholics today have no excuse for not knowing how important the Church considers the Word of God to be and, therefore, how highly they should regard it. That reverence is shown not only with incense but with use—a point often made by non-Catholics and a point we should gratefully acknowledge.

APPENDIX A

Catholic Biblical Resources

Listed below are some resources available to a beginning student of the Bible. A much more extensive list of such materials will be found in *Bible Readings and Studies: A Pastoral Bibliography* (Washington Center for the Catholic Biblical Apostolate, 1980), soon to be republished in updated form.

1. ASSOCIATIONS

These associations have a variety of materials available or can recommend study guides, periodicals, newsletters, correspondence courses, and other aids.

Paulist Evangelization Association, 3031 Fourth St. N.E., Washington, DC 20017.

U.S. Center for the Catholic Biblical Apostolate, 1312 Massachusetts Ave. N.W., Washington, DC 20005.

Rev. John Burke, O.P., Word of God Institute, 487 Michigan Ave. N.E., Washington, DC 20017.

2. PERIODICALS

Bible Sharing Newsletter, Word of God Institute, 487 Michigan Ave. N.E., Washington, DC 20017.

The Bible Today, Liturgical Press, Collegeville, MN 56321.

Discover the Bible, Bible Centre, 2000 Sherbrook St. W., Montreal, Que., Canada H3H 1G4.

God's Word Today: A Daily Guide to Reading Scripture, P.O. Box 7705, Ann Arbor, MI 48107.

Scripture in Christ, Costello Publications, Inc., P.O. Box 9, Northport, NY 11768.

Share the Word, Paulist Evangelization Association, 3031 Fourth St. N.E., Washington, DC 20017 (also available on videocassette).

The Word among Us, Box 6003, Gaithersburg, MD 20884.

3. REFERENCE WORKS

Aharoni, Yohanan, and Michael Avi-Yonah. *The Macmillan Bible Atlas*. 3d ed. New York: Macmillan, 1993.

Alexander, David and Pat, eds. *Eerdmans' Handbook to the Bible*. Grand Rapids, MI: Eerdmans, 1978.

Brown, Raymond E., Joseph A. Fitzmyer, and Roland E. Murphy, eds. *The Jerome Biblical Commentary*. Englewood Cliffs, NJ: Prentice-Hall, 1968.

Crim, Keith, ed. *The Interpreter's Dictionary of the Bible*. Nashville: Abingdon, 1976.

Hartdegen, Stephen. *Nelson's Complete Concordance of the New American Bible*. Nashville: T. Nelson, 1977.

New Catholic Study Bible, The. Huntington, IN: Our Sunday Visitor, 1985.

Reading Guides for both Testaments. Collegeville, MN: Liturgical Press.

4. INTRODUCTORY WORKS

Bivin, David, and Roy Blizzard, *Understanding the Difficult Words of Jesus: New Insights from a Hebraic Perspective*. Dayton, OH: Center for Judaic-Christian Studies, 1984.

Chapman, Charles T. *The Message of the Book of Revelation.* Collegeville, MN: Liturgical Press, 1995.

Ciuba, Edward. *Who Do You Say That I Am? An Adult Inquiry into the First Three Gospels.* New York: Alba House, 1974.

Collegeville Bible Time-Line, The. Collegeville, MN: Liturgical Press, 1993.

Duggan, Michael. *The Consuming Fire: A Christian Introduction to the Old Testament.* San Francisco: Ignatius Press, 1991.

Ellis, Peter. *The Men and the Message of the Old Testament.* Collegeville, MN: Liturgical Press, 1963.

Fuentes, A. *A Guide to the Bible.* Princeton, NJ: Scepter Press, 1987.

Gelin, Albert. *The Key Concepts of the Old Testament.* New York: Paulist Press, 1963.

Gelin, Albert. *The Religion of Israel.* New York: Hawthorne Books, 1959.

Harrington, Wilfrid. *Explaining the Gospels.* New York: Paulist Press, 1963.

Haye, George. *The Old Testament: Bible Highlights.* New York: Paulist Press, 1958.

Leon-Dufour, Xavier. *Dictionary of the New Testament.* New York: Harper and Row, 1980.

Lienhard, Joseph T. *The Bible, the Church and Authority.* Collegeville, MN: Liturgical Press, 1995.

Lukefahr, Oscar. *A Catholic Guide to the Bible.* Liguori, MO: Liguori Publications, 1992.

Mahony, Roger. *The Bible in the Life of the Catholic Church.* Collegeville, MN: Liturgical Press, 1983.

McBride, Alfred. *The Second Coming of Jesus: Meditation and Commentary on the Book of Revelation.* Huntington, IN: Our Sunday Visitor, 1993.

McKenzie, John L. *Mastering the Meaning of the Bible.* Wilkes-Barre, PA: Dimension Books, 1966.

Most, William. *The Thought of St. Paul: A Commentary on the Pauline Epistles*. Front Royal, VA: Christendom Press, 1994.

Murray, Daniel A. *The Living Word in the Living Church*. New York: Catholic Bible Press and Nelson Publishers, 1986.

National Conference of Catholic Bishops. *A Pastoral Statement for Catholics on Biblical Fundamentalism*. Washington, DC: U.S. Catholic Conference, 1987.

Navarre Bible Series, The. A multi-volume text and commentary on all the books of the New testament (Old Testament is in preparation), with Neo-Vulgate Latin and Revised Standard Version of the English; commentary consists largely of citations from the Fathers of the Church, classical spiritual writers, and magisterial sources; scholarly and theologically reliable. Scepter Publishers, P.O. Box 1270, Princeton, NJ 08542-1270.

New Jerome Bible Handbook, The. Collegeville, MN: Liturgical Press, 1992.

Parsch, Pius. *Learning to Read the Bible*. Collegeville, MN: Liturgical Press, 1963.

Pontifical Biblical Commission. *The Interpretation of the Bible in the Church*. Vatican City: Libreria Editrice Vaticana, 1993.

Sadowski, Frank. *The Church Fathers on the Bible: Selected Readings*. New York: Alba House, 1987.

Vawter, Bruce. *A Path through Genesis*. New York: Sheed & Ward, 1956.

5. AUDIO-VISUAL AIDS

Sources of audio-visual materials dealing with all aspects of the Bible: history, theology, archaeology, geography, catechetics, liturgy.

ACTA Foundation, 4848 N. Clark St., Chicago, IL 60640.

Alba House, division of the Society of St. Paul, 2187 Victory Blvd., Staten Island, NY 10314.

Daughters of St. Paul, Pauline Books and Media, 50 St. Paul's Avenue, Jamaica Plain, MA 02130.

Don Bosco Filmstrips, 148 Main Street, Box T, New Rochelle, NY 10802.

Our Sunday Visitor Publishing Division, 200 Noll Plaza, Huntington, IN 46750.

Roa's Films, 1696 N. Astor St., Milwaukee, WI 53202.

Servant Publications, Box 8617, Ann Arbor, MI 48107.

APPENDIX B

Seven Principles Essential
to Fundamentalism

When engaged in a theological discussion with Fundamentalists or other biblical literalists, Catholics need to be aware of the underlying principles given below.[1] Each principle represents a mind-set either not required by the biblical data or actually refuted by it.

1. *Regarding the nature of man:*

Man is totally corrupt. Hence there arises the tendency to limit religion to matters of sin and justification: repentance, conversion, making a decision for Christ, bewailing one's sins, condemning as evil what common experience and Catholic doctrine teach to be good (cf. CCC 405).

If this tenet is correct, what is one to make of such lines in the Scriptures as Psalm 8:5–6? "What is man that you should be mindful of him, or the son of man that you should care for him? You have made him little less than the angels, and crowned him with glory and honor." The inspired Psalmist clearly held this to be true—even after the Fall.

---

[1] These seven principles have been identified in an unpublished paper of Bartholomew de la Torre, O.P., of the Leonine Commission of The Catholic University of America, Washington, DC.

2. *Regarding the nature of grace:*

Grace is totally extrinsic. This follows from number 1, for if man is totally corrupt, then grace cannot be intrinsic to him, for then he would be transformed into something good and no longer corrupt. The blood of Christ covers over the sins of man, hiding them from the sight of God, but man remains as corrupt as before. Thus is undermined any motivation to strive to overcome vices and imperfections in oneself or in society. Indeed, the notion that man is totally corrupt and its corollary, that grace is only extrinsic, stem historically from Martin Luther's despair in trying to live the vowed life.

The grace of Christ is so powerful that Saint Paul teaches that "whoever is in Christ is a new creation" (2 Cor 5:17; CCC 1999).

3. *Regarding the nature of salvation:*

Man is saved by faith alone (cf. CCC 161–62, 2010). The way you get the blood of Christ to cover your sins is by believing that it does. Whence comes Luther's adage, "Sin strongly, but believe more strongly." When one breaks through to the conviction that, despite his inability to change, one is absolved from all responsibility, the ensuing exhilaration is the conversion experience, and the tendency is to teach that one is not saved unless one has this emotional high. Some Fundamentalists even deem one's salvation lost if this state of excitement cannot be regularly repeated.

The notion that man is saved by faith alone also means that good works are unnecessary and merit is nonexistent, in spite of the clear teaching to the contrary in James 2.

4. *Regarding the nature of the Church:*

The Church is solely an invisible society. The Church consists only of those saved by the blood of Christ. But these are only those who believe that they are so saved (see number 3). However, belief or faith is invisible. Therefore, the Church is purely and only invisible. Therefore, a visible hierarchy and also sacred images are contrary to the true faith, and the tendency is to see them as coming from the devil, with the visible (that is, Catholic) Church being seen as the Whore of Babylon and sacred images being seen as idols.

Naturally, this line of argument flies in the face of Paul's careful delineation of the Church as the Body of Christ (see 1 Cor 12; CCC 771, 779) or the Lord's own obvious intentions as recorded in Matthew 16:13–19. Hence, in the final analysis, it is a repudiation of incarnational theology.

5. *Regarding the nature of the priesthood:*

The only priesthood that exists is that common to all the faithful. Hence, both the ministerial priesthood and the Sacrifice of the Mass are denied. Since everyone in the community is hierarchically equal, the faithful have the right and, indeed, only they have the authority to select and ordain their ministers; ordination is merely the community's commission and does not in any way impart a new character or status onto the soul itself.

This Fundamentalist view derives from number 4, inasmuch as it reflects a lack of comfort with human mediation, even though many New Testament passages indicate otherwise. The story of Philip and the Ethiopian eunuch is an excellent example of a scriptural warranty for mediatory roles like preaching, authoritative interpretation of biblical texts, and a sacramental ministry (see Acts 8:26–40; CCC 1536–1600).

6. *Regarding the nature of revelation:*

The rule of faith is Scripture alone. Therefore, both Tradition and the authority of the Church to interpret are denied.

Aside from the historical record that demonstrates the opposite, even the Scriptures refute this principle. After all, Jesus promised the Holy Spirit precisely to lead His Church into all truth (see Jn 16:13), hence the need for growth and not a static situation. Also, the Gospel of John conjectures, "I do not think the whole world would contain the books that would be written" to record the words and deeds of Jesus (Jn 21:25); presumably, that statement includes the Bible as well. Further, Saint Paul encourages the Corinthians to be faithful "to the traditions, just as I handed them on to you" (1 Cor 11:2), just as he did with the Thessalonians (see 2 Th 3:6; CCC 75–82).

7. *Regarding the nature of Scripture:*

Scripture is subject only to the private interpretation of each individual. Thus man is seen as in immediate contact with revealed truth without any mediating agent other than the words of Scripture themselves. Therefore, both reason and the Church are rejected as proper channels of true interpretation. The view that man is not in need of mediation regarding the interpretation of Scripture leads to the position that man needs no mediation in any aspect of religion. Hence, not only the priesthood is seen as an intrusive interference but also the role of the angels, the saints, and Mary—even though Luther himself retained devotion to the Mother of Christ.

The insights shared in number 3 apply here as well (see CCC 85).

An Overall Evaluation:

In fact, these principles are not put into practice with consistency by any group, because they would cause too much disunity. However, these principles are adhered to verbally; if they were to be abandoned, any group still claiming to be Christian would have no logical choice but to rejoin the Catholic Church. Therefore, just because a denomination does not live up to these principles does not mean that it does not *simultaneously* proclaim them as the ideal. When listening to explanations from Fundamentalists, one needs to become aware of the presence of these principles not only directly and explicitly but especially indirectly and implicitly. If a principle is not already explicit, make it so, and then show how they themselves contradict it in practice and in theory. On the other hand, if the Fundamentalist explanation holds to the Catholic position on one or more of these seven points, agree and reinforce it.

Some Further Observations:

1. Basing herself on precisely the scriptural use of the idea of being born again or anew (e.g., Jn 3:1–5), the Catholic Church sees this event as occurring at baptism. Many Protestant denominations, especially those of the Pentecostal variety, identify being born again with the emotional exhilaration mentioned in the explanation of principle number 3, above. Scripture does not know this second meaning.

2. Historically and psychologically, the most important of the seven principles of Fundamentalism is number 1. It arose from Martin Luther's exaggerated interpretation of his own personal experiences with sin. The other six principles were developed to shore up principle number 1. However,

theologically speaking, the most important principle is number 6, and if this principle can be seen as untenable, the other six will collapse. With regard to principle number 1, the Catholic view is that everything that God has created is good (Gen 1:31), so that the mortal sinner seriously abuses, perverts, and diminishes his own goodness; but he does not totally destroy it, for he remains a creature of God. Abraham Lincoln, though a Protestant, spoke Catholic wisdom when he said, "There is so much good in the worst of us and so much bad in the best of us that it never behooves any of us to speak ill of the rest of us."

Much more can be said about each of the seven principles and about the Catholic position on each of these areas, but the above will provide a basis for further thinking and study.